Hall
in C

CLINICAL INSIGHTS

Hallucinations in Children

Edited by
DANIEL PILOWSKY, M.D.

Assistant Professor of Psychiatry, New York Medical College; Director, Child and Adolescence Inpatient Unit, Metropolitan Hospital, New York

WILLIAM CHAMBERS, M.D.

Assistant Professor of Clinical Psychiatry, Columbia University College of Physicians and Surgeons

AMERICAN PSYCHIATRIC PRESS, INC.
Washington, D.C.

Note: The authors have worked to ensure that all information in this book concerning drug dosages, schedules, and routes of administration is accurate at the time of publication and consistent with standards set by the U.S. Food and Drug Administration and the general medical community. As medical research and practice advance, however, therapeutic standards may change. For this reason and because human and mechanical errors sometimes occur, we recommend that readers follow the advice of a physician directly involved in their care or the care of a member of their family.

Copyright © 1986 American Psychiatric Press, Inc.

All Rights Reserved

Manufactured in the U.S.A.

The paper used in this publication meets the minimum requirements of American National Standard for Information Sciences—Permanence of Paper for Printed Library Materials, ANSI Z39.48-1984. ∞™

Library of Congress Cataloging in Publication Data

Main entry under title:

Hallucinations in children.

    (Clinical insights)
    Includes bibliographies.
    1. Hallucinations and illusions in children.
I. Pilowsky, Daniel, 1951–   . II. Chambers, William, 1945–   . III.
Series. [DNLM: 1. Hallucinations—in infancy & childhood.   WM 204 H193]
RJ506.H34H35   1986   155.3'088054   86-10945
ISBN 0-88048-085-8   (soft: alk. paper)

Contents

Contributors

WILLIAM CHAMBERS, M.D.
*Assistant Professor of Clinical Psychiatry, Columbia University,
College of Physicians and Surgeons*

LENORE ENGEL, M.D.
*Clinical Instructor in Psychiatry, Downstate Medical Center, State University
of New York; Director, Male Adolescent Unit, Kings County Hospital,
Brooklyn, New York*

SIDNEY KATZ, M.D.
*Clinical Professor of Psychiatry, Downstate Medical Center, State University
of New York; Director, Division of Child and Adolescent Psychiatry
Outpatient Department, Kings County Hospital, Brooklyn, New York*

DANIEL PILOWSKY, M.D.
*Assistant Professor of Psychiatry, New York Medical College; Director,
Child and Adolescence Inpatient Unit, Metropolitan Hospital, New York*

MARK PRESS, M.H.L.
*Clinical Assistant Professor of Psychiatry, Downstate Medical Center,
State University of New York; Director of Neuropsychological and
Psychoeducational Services, Division of Child and Adolescent Psychiatry,
Kings County Hospital, Brooklyn, New York*

JOHN SIMONDS, M.D.
Professor of Psychiatry, Texas Tech University Health Sciences Center

Introduction

I have a childhood memory of my own that would be absolutely splendid if it were authentic, because it goes back to an age when one doesn't usually have memories of childhood. I was still in a baby carriage, taken out by a nurse, and she took me down to the Champs-Élysées, near the Rond-Point. I was the object of an attempted kidnapping. Someone tried to grab me out of the buggy. The straps held me in and the nurse scuffled with the man, who scratched her forehead; something worse might have happened if a policeman hadn't come by just them. I can see him now as if it were yesterday—that was when they wore the little cape that comes down to here [he motions with his hand] and carried a little white stick, and all that, and the man fled. That's the story. As a child I had the glorious memory of having been the object of an attempted kidnapping. Then—I must have been about fifteen—my parents received a letter from the nurse, saying that she had just converted and wanted to confess all her sins, and that she had invented the kidnapping story herself, that she had scratched her own forehead, and that she now offered to return the watch she'd been given in recognition of her courage. In other words, there wasn't an iota of truth in the memory. And I have a very vivid memory of the experience, even today. I can tell you just where it happened in the Champs-Élysées, and I can still see the whole thing.—Jean Piaget (Bringuier 1980, p 120)

Memory and illusion, fantasy and reality, menacing trolls and fairy godmothers, the good witch of the north and the wicked witch of the west, Cheshire cats and mad hatters, human eggs and beanstalk-inhabiting giants, Mickey Mouse and the Big Bad Wolf, evil sorcerers and sage magicians, friendly ghosts and talking posts. And on and on. The mental life of children blurs the distinction between fantasy and reality, imagination and truth, actual and wished for, with determination and glee. Anna Freud and others have suggested that children's fantasy preoccupations and imaginary activities actually foster their adaptation to reality (Freud 1936; Waldre 1933). And Bleuler referred to childhood fantasy play as a normal form of the same autistic thinking he thought was pathognomonic of schizophrenia (Bleuler 1950). What, then, are we to make of the phenomenon of hallucinations reported by children?

Indeed, the question might fairly be asked whether children below a certain age can ever be considered psychotic. At one extreme, the great American child psychiatrist Lauretta Bender dealt with the issue by asserting that children could be schizophrenic without ever having been psychotic a day in their lives (Bender et al. 1952). At the other extreme, the venerable *Journal of Autism and Childhood Schizophrenia* has been renamed the *Journal of Autism and Developmental Disorders*. The latter extreme has predominated; that is, the term *childhood schizophrenia* is not listed in the *Diagnostic and Statistical Manual of Mental Disorders (Third Edition) (DSM–III;* American Psychiatric Association 1980), and currently most American child psychiatrists do not consider childhood schizophrenia an entity separate from adult schizophrenia.

Fundamental to an understanding of psychoses and psychotic phenomena is a question that is rarely asked: What are the requirements for labeling a clinical phenomenon *psychotic?* Psychoanalysts and others have argued for decades that the difference between psychotic, neurotic, and normal persons is only one of degree, whereas others have asserted that schizophrenics are different from everyone else. Strauss, Koehler, the Chapmans, and others have asserted that even hallucinations and delusions in adults are not discrete phenomena but, rather, they exist along continua ranging from normal to psychotic (Chapman and Chapman 1980). If such is the case with adults, what is one to say of hallucinations in children, in whom a suspension of reality in fantasy play is normal; in whom "hallucinated" imaginary companions are considered cute; and whose preoccupations with fantastic creatures are actively fostered by fairy tales, movies, and comic books? Children's cognitive and psychosocial immaturity reflects an incomplete development in two areas that are fundamental to the concept of psychosis: the capacities to accurately test and to adapt to reality.

It is no wonder, then, that psychotic disorders in childhood, excluding infantile autism, are among the most understudied groups of disorders in the modern age of child psychiatric research. Aside from the methodological difficulties imposed by children's immaturity on the study of childhood hallucinations and psychotic disorders is the added impediment of their relative rarity. It is an unusual center that accumulates a sufficient number of cases to make a systematic study feasible. Only a few research groups have reported on studies of schizophrenia-like psychoses in children in the last 40 years, most likely because of these difficulties.

This monograph thus represents a summary of the child psychiatric profession's work in progress. It reports on and outlines as much what is not known as what is. The concept of hallucination has been fundamental to most descriptions of psychotic conditions in this century and their diagnostic schemata, up to and including *DSM-III*. Clinicians can use this monograph as a guide through the diagnostic pitfalls of one of our most challenging disorders or group of disorders: the psychoses, and especially the psychoses of childhood.

This monograph includes a discussion of the clinical assessment of children who present with hallucinations (Chapter 1), and a discussion of the diagnostic evaluation of these children (Chapters 2 and 3). The biological and the psychoanalytic aspects of hallucinatory phenomena are dealt with in Chapters 4 and 5, respectively.

There are two major differences between hallucinatory phenomena in childhood and the same phenomena in adulthood. The first major difference is that it is more difficult to determine whether a child is hallucinating. This is a problem of clinical assessment. The second difference is that the diagnostic implications of the presence of hallucinations are more complex and varied in children than in adults. This is a problem of diagnosis.

What makes the clinical assessment of a child who presents with hallucinations different from the assessment of an adult with the same type of symptom? The presence of hallucinations implies a failure of consensual validation. Children normally develop the capacities and abilities that underlie consensual validation in a gradual fashion. Therefore, in young normal children these abilities and capacities may not yet be fully developed. The developmental issues that underlie the clinical assessment of these children are discussed in some detail in Chapter 1, and throughout this monograph.

What makes the diagnosis of these children more complicated than the diagnosis of adults who present with hallucinations? The presence of hallucinations in adults is usually considered to be part of a psychotic process. This issue is not as clear in children. Descriptions of hallucinations in nonpsychotic children are relatively common in the pediatric psychiatric literature. These issues, and other issues that arise in the course of the diagnostic evaluation of children who hallucinate, are discussed in Chapter 2O.

The diagnostic issues that arise in the evaluation of nonorganic (that is, without a diagnosed organic brain syndrome) psychotic and depressed children who hallucinate are discussed separately in Chapter 3O. The classification, course, and prognosis of psychoses in childhood are known to be controversial and poorly understood topics. The diagnostic issues that arise in the evaluation of psychotic children who hallucinate cannot be separated from the controversy regarding the psychoses of childhood. Therefore, the reader will find in Chapter 3 a summary of this controversy.

The next chapter, Chapter 4, deals with the biological mechanisms that underlie hallucinatory phenomena. The authors attempt to cover the neurophysiological and neurochemical investigations of hallucinatory states. They examine dream states, drug-induced hallucinations, amphetamine psychoses, and hallucinatory experiences in some nonfunctional illnesses. They place particular emphasis on the role of serotonin and its interaction with other neurotransmitters. Chapter 4 also includes a brief review of some theories of the cognitive and perceptual mechanisms underlying hallucinations. Most of the biological studies on hallucinations emanate from the adult psychiatric literature. Given the absence of similar studies in the child literature, this chapter is based mostly on reports of biological research in adults. Modern biological psychiatry attempts to bridge the gap between psychological and biological mechanisms. In line with this spirit, some of the biological theories of hallucinations are used to discuss the relationship between psychological stress and the presence of hallucinations in terms of an interactive model. Slade's model, discussed in Chapter 4, is clearly such a model, involving the interaction of constitutional, environmental, and experiential dimensions.

The last chapter, Chapter 5, deals with hallucinatory phenomena from a psychoanalytic vantage point. Numerous authors have attempted to classify hallucinatory phenomena both in children and in adults from a psychoanalytic point of view. Each one of these attempts emphasizes a different aspect of the same phenomena, which has resulted in a confusing mass of literature. Here an attempt is made to integrate these diverse contributions.

The editors and contributors intend this volume to constitute a comprehensive panorama of the current knowledge in childhood hallucinations. We also hope to convey an understanding of the complexities and controversies that arise in this area, where numerous issues are poorly understood and in need of clarification.

Daniel Pilowsky, M.D.
William Chambers, M.D.

References

American Psychiatric Association: Diagnostic and Statistical Manual of Mental Disorders (Third Edition). Washington, DC, American Psychiatric Association, 1980

Bender L, Friedman AM, Grugett AE, et al: Schizophrenia in childhood—a confirmation of the diagnosis. Transactions of the American Neurological Association 77:67–93, 1952

Bleuler E: Dementia Praecox or the Group of the Schizophrenias. New York, International Universities Press, 1950

Bringuier JC: Conversations With Jean Piaget. Chicago, University of Chicago Press, 1980

Chapman L, Chapman J: Scales for rating psychotic and psychotic-like experiences as continua. Schizophr Bull 6:476–489, 1980

Freud A: The Ego and the Mechanisms of Defense. New York, International Universities Press, 1936

Waldre R: Psychoanalytic theory of play. Psychoanal Q 2:208–224, 1933

1

Problems in Determining the Presence of Hallucinations in Children

Daniel Pilowsky, M.D.

1

Problems in Determining the Presence of Hallucinations in Children

When examining children, clinicians are often asked to determine whether a child is hallucinating. In this chapter, we focus on the phenomenological distinction between hallucinations and parahallucinatory phenomena. Parahallucinatory experiences are either hallucinatory perceptions that are present in normal development—that is, hypnogogic and hypnopompic hallucinations—or instances of vivid imagination that bear apparent similarity to hallucinations, such as eidetic imagery, imaginary companions, and other related experiences. Clearly the determination of the presence of hallucinations often has major clinical implications in terms of severity of psychopathology, differential diagnosis, and therapeutic interventions. These areas are addressed in Chapters 2 and 3.

It is often assumed that there is a dichotomous yes-or-no answer to the question of whether a child is hallucinating. This assumption is questionable. In my experiences examining children, I have noticed a spectrum of phenomena. At one end of the spectrum are instances of vivid imagination, such as eidetic imagery, imaginary companions, and so forth. The other end consists of clear-cut hallucinations. Between these two extremes is a gray area that includes those cases where it cannot be determined with a reasonable degree of certainty whether a child is hallucinating. I postulate that looking at other areas of the child's functioning is the key to evaluating these children.

DEVELOPMENTAL CONSIDERATIONS

By definition we can use the term *hallucination* as a meaningful construct only after the child has learned to distinguish between the internal world and external reality. As Rothstein (1981) points out, there is disagreement as to the age at which this distinction is sufficiently stable to preclude hallucinatory phenomena in normal children. Despert (1948) claims that the normal child of average intelligence is fully able to distinguish between fantasy and reality by the age of three years. Whatever that age limit might be, the question of hallucinations is not a meaningful one before that time. The problem of reality testing, the limitations of the child's vocabulary, and the egocentric frame of reference of the young child compound the complexity of the assessment. Piaget (1962) suggested that in the earlier portion of the years between four and six, a significant proportion of speech is egocentric. *Egocentric*, as used by Piaget, means that the child is centered about him- or herself and fails to take into account the other's point of view. A child this age may talk about products of his or her imagination without referring to their imaginary nature. The child assumes that it is understood and thus does not trouble to be explicit about it. It is the interviewer's task to help the child make this distinction. The child may ascribe private meanings to certain words or expressions. The existence of these meanings is incompatible with the consensually validated logic of the adult. Therefore, as Eisenberg (1962, p 201) points out, "Care is necessary in analyzing communications from the young child lest we read into them our own meanings."

Another aspect of Piaget's work might be relevant to our task: the distinction that the child makes between dreams and reality (Piaget 1962). This distinction may be considered analogous to the distinction between the internal world and external reality. It has already been suggested in this chapter that the concept of hallucinations becomes meaningful only after the child is able to distinguish between the internal world and external reality. Therefore, it is suggested that children would be able to distinguish between hallucinations and products of their imagination around the time when they start separating dreams from reality. Piaget suggests that up to the age of three years, dreams are confused with reality. After that age, children admit that dreams are not real, but they still believe that dreams exist in the room as visible pictures. At about the age of six, children cease to believe in the external quality of dreams and discover that they are in one's mind. If the dream reality distinction is indeed parallel to the hallucination fantasy distinction, one would question the application of the term *hallucination* prior to the age of six.

The postulated parallel between dreams and hallucinations requires further consideration. In discussing dreams, Piaget (1962) stated:

> The sleeper is still conscious of something, since he is dreaming, but he is not conscious of the ego, since he is not aware that he is asleep nor that he is dreaming. Even when he himself is part of his dream, it is through a kind of projection similar to that of children who talk about themselves in the third person. It is not consciousness of his present subjective activity, but an imaged story in which he is one of the characters. (p 201)

I shall paraphrase Piaget by stating that people who hallucinate are conscious of something, since they are hallucinating, but they are not aware that they are in an altered state of mind; that is, they are not aware that they are hallucinating. Piaget (1962) mentions other features of dreams that can be construed as parallel to the hallucinatory experience:

> Moreover, it is clear that in dreams the absence of consciousness of the ego entails the kind of immediate belief that is prior even to the possibility of doubt, while in play this belief gradually gives way to the feeling of make-believe, for reasons that we have seen. (p 202)

The kind of immediate belief that excludes the possibility of doubting is exactly what is seen in clear-cut hallucinations. This feature of hallucinations, which will later be referred to as *cre-*

dence in the hallucinations, constitutes the basis of one of the criteria that is used in distinguishing hallucinations from fantasy-related phenomena. This point will be discussed in the clinical section of this chapter. In sum, many of the features that Piaget attributes to dreams may also be attributed to hallucinations.

So far we have seen how developmental issues are to be considered in order to avoid labeling a child's experience as hallucinating when the child is not hallucinating. Edgell and Kolvin (1972) have suggested that the opposite may take place. The clinician may be led to believe that a child is not hallucinating when the child is indeed doing so. The following factors may account for such a belief: the child's variability in attention and memory, changes in consciousness or affect, attitude toward the interviewer, expectations, wishes to comply or to resist, and situational anxieties. At times a child may deliberately withhold information about his or her hallucinations as a result of very specific situational anxieties, such as the fear of being hospitalized and thus separated from the parents or the fear of admitting to "bad thoughts" when the content of the hallucinations is of an aggressive or sexual nature.

HALLUCINATIONS AND PARAHALLUCINATORY PHENOMENA

Most authors have used a definition of hallucination that is similar to that offered by Hinsie and Campbell (1970): "an apparent perception of an external object when no such object is present" (p 333). Edgell and Kolvin (1972) have pointed out that such definitions do not clearly distinguish between hallucinations and parahallucinatory phenomena or vivid imagery, which are particularly important in children. The above definition does not include any reference to the developmental stage or the cognitive development of the individual. As parahallucinatory phenomena are discussed, it will become apparent that perceptions, without the presence of an external object, are a frequent occurrence in normal children. Several forms of parahallucinatory phenomena are to be considered in all children who might be hallucinating.

Eidetic Imagery

Eidetic imagery is the ability to produce vivid visual images that are not confused with reality. Anthony (1959) describes a decreasing incidence with age from 60% at age four to 7% in adults. Other authors have found a significantly lower incidence (Haber and Haber 1964). Be that as it may, it is important to keep in mind that eidetic imagery is fairly common in preschool children without any neurotic symptoms or emotional maladjustments. The affected children, as in the case of imaginary companions, are aware of the unreality of their experiences.

Imaginary Companions

In a classic paper, Bender (1941) described the imaginary companions of children. According to Bender they are often found in nonpsychotic children, with the highest incidence among lonely children. These children can clearly distinguish between their imaginary friends and their real ones; that is, they do not believe in the external reality of their imaginary friends and they are subjectively aware of these friends' imaginary nature. This phenomenon is considered normal by most authors. The children described by Bender were between 5 and 10 years of age. Some investigators have reported that children who have imaginary companions are more intelligent and/or more creative than those who do not. However, only two studies (Jersild et al. 1933; Svendsen 1934) contain findings to support the contention that children who are able to describe an imaginary companion are more intelligent. Others (Bairdain 1959; Singer 1961) failed to demonstrate such a difference. A recent study (Manosewitz et al. 1977) attempted to verify these assumptions. These researchers were unable to demonstrate statistically significant differences of intelligence or creativity between a group of children who had imaginary companions and a group of children who did not. In summary, no specific features distinguish this group of children from their counterparts who do not have imaginary companions.

Hypnogogic and Hypnopompic Hallucinations

Hallucinations that take place while falling asleep (hypnogogic) and while waking up (hypnopompic) are normal physiological phenomena. The clinician can easily distinguish them according to their relationship to the state of sleep.

Dreams and Night Terrors

I have included night terrors and dreams in this section because children may refer to dreamed voices or images without spontaneously revealing that they are referring to dream material. It is suggested that clinicians ask young children who report having hallucinations whether they occurred when sleeping or dreaming.

Night terrors, or *pavor nocturnus*, are characterized by intense anxiety. Typically, the child wakes up screaming and crying for help, appears relatively unresponsive to the environment, and may be delusional or hallucinating. Night terrors are also characterized by greatly increased manifestations of autonomic disturbance; that is, increased heart rate and increased respiratory rate. Within minutes the high levels of autonomic activity subside and the child can be helped to return to bed and sleep.

We now know that night terrors occur during arousal from slow-wave Stage 4 sleep, whereas nightmares or anxiety dreams occur during rapid eye movement (REM) periods. The onset of night terrors can frequently be traced to the recent occurrence of a traumatic event, such as a separation from the parents, a hospitalization, or the death of a family member.

CLINICAL ASSESSMENT

One goal of the clinical interview is to help the clinician make a phenomenological distinction between hallucinatory and parahallucinatory experiences. This distinction is based either on direct observation of children who hallucinate or on reports of hallucinatory experiences provided by the child and the child's family. Because direct observation is often unavailable to the clinician, these reports are frequently the only source of data. If direct observation were possible, clinicians would be able to assess the child's degree of involvement with internal stimuli and the degree of interference with reality testing, adaptation, and judgment. Nevertheless, the phenomenological distinction is difficult even when direct observation is possible. This section will deal with the clinician's approach to children who may be hallucinating, focusing mostly on reports of hallucinations provided by these children.

In the clinical interview the first task is to help the child feel free to discuss these often frightening experiences. Despert (1948) suggests that the clinician should reassure each child that all children might have experiences such as those being discussed. Lukianowicz (1969) has expressed the concern that attention-seeking children might claim hallucinations that they in fact have never experienced. He suggested that spontaneous reports are more reliable than reports elicited through questioning the child. My suggestion is that while one should be reassuring, one should also be careful not to put words into the child's mouth. In the course of the interview, the clinician may discuss dreams, daydreams, and imagery with the child. Before asking about hallucinations proper, following the example of Aug and Ables (1971), the difference between "real" and "make-believe" or "pretend" should be demonstrated. If asked to examine a six-year-old boy who "sees things," one may ask the boy to close his eyes and picture an object in his mind. Let us assume that the boy tells the interviewer that he pictured a lion that he recently saw in the local zoo. At this point the boy would be asked to compare that pretend image with the appearance of several objects present in the room, such as a chair or telephone. The question may be phrased as follows: "Are the things that you see at home like the chair or the telephone that you see here in the office, or like the make-believe lion that you just saw when you closed you eyes?" A similar paradigm may be used for hallucinations in modalities other than visual. At this point the child would be prepared to discuss hallucinations proper.

When the child is questioned about hallucinations proper, I use a set of criteria that may be helpful in distinguishing hallucinations from the parahallucinatory phenomena described above.

These criteria are derived from the literature (Aug and Ables 1971; Lukianowicz 1969; Rothstein 1981) and from clinical experience.

Vividness of the Hallucinations

It is suggested that the degree of vividness of the hallucinations be evaluated. Here one is dealing with a sense that the perception itself, and not necessarily the object perceived, is real. The child may be asked if the hallucinated voice is heard in the same way he or she hears the clinician's voice or if the voice sounds like the voice of a "real person." If there is a question of visual hallucinations, the clinician may ask the child if the pictures look like pictures in "real life" or like "make-believe" pictures. Retarded children, who tend to be very concrete, may find it difficult to grasp this distinction.

Credence in the Hallucinations

Here one is dealing with the immediate sense of certainty that what is perceived is an object actually present. In other words, there is a belief in the external reality of the perceived object. In the case of a girl who sees a monster in her room, the clinician could ask her whether she could touch it. In the case of a boy who reports that he sees a big man, the boy could be asked whether he could shake the hand of the big man. If a child acts on a hallucination, the clinician may assume that the child gives it credence. The child's affect is also relevant. If a child is observed while he or she is hallucinating, the affect may be observed directly. For example, if a girl tells the interviewer that she sees a large, frightening mouse in the room at that very moment, the examiner is able to observe whether the girl seems frightened or calm. Of course, in the latter case, the girl would not be acting like a child who gives credence to the hallucination. The opposite would be true if the child became terrified or panicky. Reports of relatives who have seen the child while hallucinating may be another helpful way of assessing the child's affective reaction to the hallucinatory experience. However, hallucinations that have been perceived for long periods of time may not elicit a panic response.

Ego-Alien Source of Hallucinations

A source of hallucinations is ego-alien if it appears to be other than the patient's own subjective experience or if it appears to be beyond the limits of his or her internal world. Should the source of the perception be ego-alien, such a perception is more likely to be a hallucination. On the other hand, if the source of the perception is not ego-alien, that is, if the child believes that the source of the perception is in his or her own internal world, such a perception is less likely to be a hallucination. This dimension is difficult to evaluate during the clinical interview. Some children might be able to convey that the perception is not ego-alien by saying, "The voice of the man I hear is in my own head" or "It must come from myself." On the other hand, if a child reports hearing the voice of a man and states that the voice must come from wherever the man is located, then the perception is clearly ego-alien because the child believes that the source of the hallucination is not in his or her own internal world. In both cases, the child hears the voice of a man. However, in the first case, the child believes that the voice emanates from his or her own subjective experience, whereas in the second, the child believes that the voice emanates from a source other than the internal world.

Volitional Quality of the Hallucinations

This problem may be formulated as follows: Does the clinician sense that the hallucinations are under the voluntary control of the child? Is the child able to control the emergence and content of the hallucinations? The clinician may ask the child if he or she can make the voices or images "appear and disappear" whenever the child "wants to." In the case of visual images, one may ask, "Can you make the picture look nice?" or "Can you see anything you want to?" or "Can you stop them?" These questions about visual imagery may be helpful in distinguishing eidetic imagery from visual hallucinations.

It is clear that these four criteria constitute overlapping categories that can be separated only for didactic purposes. None of the

four criteria outlined above are to be considered in isolation. However, it is suggested that, considered jointly, they may be helpful in
distinguishing hallucinations from parahallucinatory phenomena
and other fantasy-related phenomena.

Case Study 1

A seven-year-old boy named Jack was admitted to a city hospital after
he told his teacher that he was going to jump out of the window
because the devil told him to do so. The child had actually walked
toward the window when the teacher intervened. This boy had mentioned hearing the voice of the devil on previous occasions. A short
time prior to his admission to the hospital, he had written a few words
on his desk in school. The teacher questioned Jack about this behavior. Jack stated that he had done what the devil had told him to do.
    When interviewed at the hospital the topic of the hallucinations
was introduced by telling Jack that the school had informed the
interviewer of his wish to jump out of the window. Jack confirmed
the information received from the school. The child was asked where
the idea of jumping came from. His answer was "the devil." Jack was
then asked to give a detailed description of the devil's communications. Jack said, "He talks to me, I hear him like I hear you, but his
voice comes from far away." At this point Jack was asked whether it
was a "real devil" or a "make-believe devil." Jack replied, "He has a
voice like you." When asked about the location of the devil, Jack
replied, "at home," stated that the devil was real, and proceeded to
describe him as follows: "He looks black, he looks crazy, he smells
pickley." Jack also told the interviewer that the devil instructed him
not only to jump out of the window but also to do trivial things, such
as stand up, play with dolls, and so forth. Jack was then asked if he had
heard the devil that day. Jack reported that the devil had asked him if
he needed any help. Finally, Jack was asked if he felt funny hearing
the devil talking to him. He replied, "I don't care."

This interview will be discussed in light of the four criteria
outlined above. Jack conveyed the sense that he experienced the
perception of the devil as real when he stated that he heard the
devil's voice in the same way that he heard the interviewer's
voice. Therefore, it was concluded that Jack experienced the hallucinations vividly.

This boy also gave credence to the hallucinations. This was
manifested by his belief in the external objectivity of the devil. In

other words, he believed that there was an actual devil that talked to him, as opposed to a make-believe one. It follows that this boy did not experience the devil as part of his internal world; hence, the hallucinatory experience was ego-alien. Finally, Jack reported that he could not bring about the hallucinations at will, that, on the contrary, the hallucinations were experienced as an unexpected intrusion. Therefore, Jack did not have volitional control of the hallucinations.

In summary, Jack perceived the hallucinations vividly, gave them credence, experienced them as ego-alien, and had no volitional control of them. It was concluded that Jack was clearly hallucinating.

Case Study 2

A seven-year-old girl was referred for psychiatric evaluation by a pediatrician because of anorexia. During the clinical interview the girl reported hearing voices of children saying that she was "too thin." The girl was a verbal, intelligent, and engaging child. The following dialogue took place in the course of her evaluation:

Clinician: Do you hear the voices when you are with other kids or when you are by yourself?
Girl: When I'm alone in my room.
Clinician: Do you hear them at night when you are sleeping or when you are about to fall asleep?
Girl: Sometimes.
Clinician: Any other times?
Girl: Other times it is in the middle of the day, when I'm in school. [Notice that so far dreams and hypnogogic and hypnopompic hallucinations have been ruled out.]
Clinician: Can other people hear it?
Girl: No.
Clinician: How come?
Girl: Because I have bionic ears.
Clinician: Where do the voices come from?
Girl: Kids. I don't know who they are. [At this point the clinician had noticed that the little girl was delighted to tell about the voices. The clinician kept in mind the possibility that this might be an attention-seeking device.]
Clinician: Can you make them come and go?
Girl: Yes, because I have bionic ears like the bionic woman. [Notice

that the child seems to have volitional control of the hallucinations. She also seems influenced by a popular television program.]

Clinician: Are they real or make-believe?

Girl: I really hear them. I told you I got bionic ears. [The girl believes it's an actual perception.]

In this case, the four criteria—vividness, credence, whether the source is ego-alien, and volitional quality—some are filled and some are not. This girl seems to have volitional control of the hallucinations, as shown by the statement "I can make them come and go." Given the presence of volitional control, one might conclude that this girl may not be truly hallucinating. However, all four criteria should be considered. In considering the vividness of the hallucinations, it becomes clear that for this girl the hallucinations were vivid. She experienced them as an actual perception. If this criterion were considered in isolation, one would conclude that the girl was truly hallucinating.

If the hallucinated voices were part of the child's internal world, the experience would not be considered ego-alien. In this case the description of the experience by the patient was ambiguous: The girl simply stated that she heard kids' voices, and she was not sure whether they were "in my own head" or "real kids in the neighborhood." Further questioning was not helpful.

In summary, applying the four criteria does not allow the clinician to reach a clear conclusion. It was suggested earlier that hallucinatory phenomena could be understood in terms of a spectrum that ranges from vivid imagination to clear-cut hallucinations. In the example just discussed, the girl's experience seems to fall in the middle. This is not an infrequent occurrence. It is suggested that in such cases the clinician explore other aspects of the child's ego functions. In the case of this girl, no other evidence of impaired reality testing was found. Psychiatric treatment was recommended because this girl was also anorexic and socially isolated from her peers. This recommendation was not based solely on the presence of the possible hallucinations. Similar phenomena in a child whose overall functioning was unimpaired (not the case here) might have led to the recommendation that immediate treatment was not indicated. One might recommend in such a case that a second evaluation be conducted a few months later. I want to emphasize that it may neither be possible nor be essential at this point in the child's assessment to arrive at a definite conclusion concerning hallucinations.

DEFINITION OF HALLUCINATION REVISED

The definition of hallucination most often used ("an apparent perception of an external object when no such object is present") does not clearly distinguish between children who hallucinate and children who report any of the parahallucinatory phenomena described above. Rothstein (1981) dealt with this problem by narrowing down the definition of hallucination. She suggested:

> Careful consideration of the phenomenology of the child's experience and his developmental capacities must lead to the firm conclusion that the child is perceiving something that is not there, that he is not in a sleep or presleep state, and that he is unable to reflect upon its lack of external objectivity. (p 633)

In contrast to Rothstein's suggestion, I believe that even after careful consideration of the phenomenology of the child's experience, it may remain unclear whether the child is truly hallucinating. It is at times unclear whether the child is able to reflect on "the lack of external objectivity." This difficulty may be based not only on the child's limited descriptive ability but also on the continuity between vivid fantasies and hallucinations. It is suggested here that these are not two distinct categories but that they constitute two ends of a spectrum of phenomena with many intermediate states. This suggestion emanates from a general hypothesis regarding the continuity of mental phenomena (Savage 1975). This hypothesis states that hallucinations, fantasies, dreams, and thoughts are not sharply distinguishable from one another and that the experiences may evolve one into another. This hypothesis is, in my opinion, especially relevant to young children. From this vantage point a definitive distinction between vivid fantasies and hallucinations is no longer valid. What then should the clinician do? It is suggested here that he or she must first evaluate the child to ascertain whether the hallucinations fall near either end of the spectrum. The use of the four criteria outlined above may be helpful in making this evaluation. It is understood that the clinician will always evaluate the child more completely by including an assessment of the child's ego functions, cultural background, developmental stage, and so on. Only at this point can the clinician arrive at a meaningful conclusion.

Before closing, a few words about cultural background as it relates to children's hallucinations: In certain cultures some hallucinatory experiences, such as hearing voices of dead relatives, are fairly common. These experiences, if reported by a child living in that culture, would receive consensual validation from the adults in the family. If the child's hallucinations are syntonic with the beliefs of his or her culture, the clinician should consider carefully the role of the culture before making a judgment about the presence and the pathological significance of the hallucinations.

References

Anthony J: An experimental approach to the psychopathology of childhood: sleep disturbances. Br J Med Psychol 32:19–37, 1959

Aug R, Ables B: Hallucinations in nonpsychotic children. Child Psychiatry Hum Dev 1:153–167, 1971

Bairdain EF: Psychological characteristics of adolescents who have had imaginary companions. Dissertation Abstracts International 29:747, 1959

Bender L, Fogel FB: Imaginary companions of children. Am J Orthopsychiatry 11:56–65, 1941

Despert JL: Delusional and hallucinatory experiences in children. Am J Psychiatry 104:528–537, 1948

Edgell HG, Kolvin I: Childhood hallucinations. J Child Psychol Psychiatry 13:279–287, 1972

Eisenberg L: Hallucinations in children, in Hallucinations. Edited by West LJ. New York, Grune and Stratton, 1962, 198–207

Haber RN, Haber RE: Eidetic imagery frequency. Percept Mot Skills 19:131–138, 1964

Hinsie LE, Campbell RJ: Psychiatric Dictionary, 4th ed. New York, Oxford University Press, 1970

Jersild AT, Markey FV, Jersild CL: Children's fears, dreams, wishes, daydreams, likes, dislikes, pleasant and unpleasant memories. Child Development Monograph 12. New York, Teachers College, Columbia University, 1933

Lukianowicz N: Hallucinations in nonpsychotic children. Psychiat Clin (Basel) 2:321–337, 1969

Manosewitz M, Fling S, Prentice NM: Imaginary companions in young children: Relationships with intelligence, creativity and writing ability. J Child Psychol Psychiatry 18:73–78, 1977

Piaget J: Play Dreams and Imitation in Childhood. New York, WW Norton, 1962

Rothstein A: Hallucinatory phenomena in childhood. J Am Acad Child Psychiatry 20:623–635, 1981

Savage CW: The continuity of perceptual and cognitive experiences, in Hallucination. Edited by Siegel RK, West LJ. New York, Wiley, 1975

Singer JL: Imagination and writing ability in young children. Journal of Personality 29:396–413, 1961

Svendsen M: Children's imaginary companions. Archives of Neurological Psychiatry 32:985–999, 1934

2

Hallucinations in Children: Diagnostic Considerations

John Simonds, M.D.

2

Hallucinations in Children: Diagnostic Considerations

The diagnostic and psychodynamic aspects of hallucinations in children, including the various organic and psychiatric disorders that can present with hallucinatory phenomena, are the subjects of this chapter. Any discussion about hallucinations needs to be introduced with a definition and classification system. I will primarily refer to Horowitz's (1975) information processing model in describing hallucinations. According to Horowitz (1975), a hallucination is "an image experience in which there is a discrepancy between subjective experience and actual reality" (p 167). The hallucinator experiences him- or herself and acts as if he or she were perceiving through the various senses. Hallucinations derive from internal sources but are appraised incorrectly as coming from outside sources. Usually the images are regarded as strange and as having intruded into awareness without intention. Adults project their hallucinations to the outside world, but most children tend to experience hallucinations as occurring within the self.

The characteristics of hallucinations described above are "ideal," but most hallucinations are far from ideal. There is often a transition from thought images to hallucinations; for example, the experience progresses from warded-off fantasy images to more intrusive images that are eventually appraised as quasi-real and later experienced as vivid images that the individual cognitively knows are not real and, finally, to images to which the individual reacts as if they were real (Horowitz 1975). Another type of progression described by Horowitz is the gradual loss of differentiation between external and internal sources of information; for example, blurring images become vivid geometric designs and finally elaborate images. In considering auditory hallucinations, there can be a continuum from having silent thoughts to hearing one's thoughts spoken aloud to hearing voices from outside and, finally, to engaging in conversation with voices.

According to the information processing model for hallucinations (Horowitz 1975), the image system of representation (in contrast to the lexical system of representation) can be activated by electrochemical stimulation anywhere along the sensory tracts to the cortex or by psychological changes. Sudden or intense emergence of ideas and emotions related to fear or self-aims can activate the image system rather than the lexical system. Images substitute quite easily for external objects when there is such a need. Some individuals think primarily in terms of images and some can turn on visual images at will, whereas other individuals are primarily lexicon thinkers. Horowitz (1975) postulated that persons not accustomed to the image system of representation are more likely to describe such an experience as a hallucination.

Another determinant of the hallucinatory experience stresses the intensification of internal input into the image system of representation. According to Horowitz (1975), this would occur under the following circumstances: a) relative reduction of external input with no relative lowering of receptivity, such as sensory deprivation; b) increase in the activity of the image representational system without increase in external stimulation, such as hallucinations related to brain stimulation; c) augmentation of internal input due to arousal of ideas and feelings secondary to wishes, needs, and/or fear states, such as hallucinations of a lost relative; d) reduction in the usual levels of inhibition over internal inputs, such as hypnogogic hallucinations; and e) alteration of the transition between matrices (which operate to process information from sources such as perception, memory, or fantasy) so that internal inputs gain more representation on matrices oriented toward perception, such as ambiguous perceptions becoming vivid internal elaborations (for example, monsters in a dark room).

Impaired information processing can also account for experiencing or labeling dim or fleeting images as hallucinations (Horowitz 1975). States of general cognitive impairment, high conflict, stress, or the need for fantasy gratifications increase the likelihood of such occurrences. Sometimes disruptions in short-term memory can lead to retrospective hallucinations.

Sudden lapses in control over internal input to the image system can also result in intrusive image experiences (Horowitz 1975). This can occur as a sequel to stressful perceptions, as eruptive representations of usually warded off ideas and feelings not related to the stress, and as a result of defenses aimed at the transformation of affective states (for example, a grieving person relieves his sadness by hallucinating a replica of a dead relative).

It is difficult to distinguish when a child is experiencing a true hallucination. Certain aspects of child development and family background can impair the process of differentiating subjective imagery from actual experiencing. Aug and Ables (1971) summarized some of these factors in terms of developmental limitations that may predispose the child to experience hallucinations:

1. Age and limited intelligence are very important limiting factors. For a child, wish-fulfilling fantasy is a common mode of thinking. However, a child of average intelligence at age three years can usually distinguish between fantasy and reality.
2. Emotional deprivation can also lead to increased fantasy thinking, and perhaps hallucinations, as a way of providing the gratifications that reality cannot provide.
3. Emphasis of a particular mode of perception because of life experience may make it difficult to distinguish between vivid auditory imagery and auditory hallucinations in a partially deaf child or visual imagery and visual hallucinations in a child whose parent is preoccupied about the health of the eyes.
4. Family religious and/or cultural beliefs may predispose children to have deviant perceptual experiences (for example, Pentecostal religious experiences).

5. Strong emotional states at times of stress may lead to regression and hallucinations.

Weiner (1961) differentiated between primary hallucinations occurring in the absence of a diagnosable disease or disorder and secondary hallucinations occurring during the course of an organic or functional psychiatric disorder. Primary hallucinations include: a) hypnogogic hallucinations (transient hallucinations in the twilight between waking and true sleep); b) eidetic imagery (the ability to visualize or auditorize an object long after it has been seen or heard; children normally possess this ability but lose it gradually as they approach puberty); c) imaginary playmate (a distinct person who occupies space and can be a companion particularly for three- to five-year-olds; the child who has an imaginary companion is quite aware of the unreality of the phenomenon); d) dreams; e) isolated hallucinations (fleeting illusions based on misinterpretation of shadows, colors, and movements); and f) hallucinosis (a number of hallucinations extending over a period of time but not related to any known cause).

The focus of this chapter is on the so-called secondary type of hallucinations rather than the above-mentioned primary type of hallucinations, which can occur normally in any child.

Before reviewing the various disorders associated with hallucinations, I thought it would be important to state that hallucinations are just as likely to occur in nonpsychotic conditions as in psychotic conditions. Many reports from the literature support this viewpoint. The 4 boys about whom Levin (1932) wrote experienced auditory hallucinations in the midst of family crises and personality problems. In 1948 Despert reported on the case histories of 3 children who had auditory hallucinations related to anxiety, guilt, and atonement issues. Wilking and Paoli (1966) observed 42 nonpsychotic children with hallucinations associated primarily with anxiety, deprivation, neurotic conflict, and organicity. Esman's (1962) 5 cases of visual hallucinosis had acute anxiety and maturational irregularities. Lukianowicz (1969) studied the hallucinations of 14 children who spontaneously described hallucinatory experiences. Anxiety states, grief, and depression were common themes in these children's histories. In Simonds's (1975) study of 10 nonpsychotic children, 8 had prominent depressive features and 7 had prominent anxiety related to school and family stress. Garralda (1982) reported that 20 children with nonpsychotic hallucinations had experienced primarily auditory hallucinations commanding the child to do something bad; the stress was often related to a bereavement process.

ORGANIC AND FUNCTIONAL DISORDERS ASSOCIATED WITH HALLUCINATIONS

Delirium (Acute Organic Brain Syndrome)

In children this syndrome has manifestations similar to adult delirium, that is, disorientation, disturbed attention and concentration, impaired memory, agitation, restlessness, disturbed sleep cycle, and hallucinations that are commonly visual. Hallucinations can occur during any febrile illness but are more frequent during typhoid fever, scarlet fever, influenza, and peneumonia. Even after the fever has subsided, there may be episodes of hallucinations (Weiner 1961).

Nutritional deficiency states such as starvation, beriberi, and pellagra (Weiner 1961), and metabolic disorders such as adrenocortical hypofunction, thyroid disorders, parathyroid disorders, vitamin D intoxication, and hypomagnesemia (Lewis 1982) can result in hallucinations with associated delirium. Case reports of hallucinations following hyperventilation in teenagers (Allen and Agus 1968) were speculated to be related to vasoconstriction of cerebral vessels. During hypoglycemic states there is usually confusion, weakness, sweating, hunger, and headaches. In rare instances hallucinations can occur (Weiner 1961). Head trauma (Laufer and Shetty 1979; Weiner 1961), encephalitis, meningitis (Lewis 1982), and encephalopathies associated with uremia, heart failure, anoxia, and porphyria (Weiner 1961) have also been implicated in some cases of hallucinations with delirium. Systemic lupus erythematosus, which affects the central nervous system, may present with visual hallucinations as well as affective and other organic brain symptoms (Silber et al. 1984).

The most significant groups of disorders with delirium are the toxic and drug-induced disorders. In addition to the usual symptoms of delirium, patients with drug-induced syndromes may manifest suggestibility and neurological dysfunctions such as ataxia, tremors, dyskinesia, dysarthria, and dilated pupils. Drugs associated with delirium and hallucinations include:

1. Nitrous oxide (anesthetic) can cause hyperacusis, delirium, and excitement, especially if oxygen supply is limited (Frost 1985).
2. Ketamine (anesthetic) produces a dissociation between the limbic system and the thalamocortical pathways. Hallucinations involve bright colors and shapes. The frequency is dose related and can be modified by intravenous diazepam (Cunningham and McKinney 1983).
3. Anthihistamines (e.g., tripelennamine) when taken in large doses are common causes of hallucinations in children (Connell 1977; Medical Letter on Drugs and Therapeutics 1981).
4. Barbiturates (such as phenobarbital) can cause excitement, hyperactivity, depression, delirium and visual hallucinations not only upon withdrawal but with usual doses in some children (Medical Letter on Drugs and Therapeutics 1981).
5. Bromides can produce terrifying hallucinations, especially at night (Kaplan and Sadock 1981).
6. Anticonvulsant medications (such as dilantin) in high doses can be associated with delirium and auditory, tactile, and visual hallucinations (Medical Letter on Drugs and Therapeutics 1981).
7. Atropine and other anticholinergic drugs at higher doses are frequent precipitants of confusion, disorientation, depersonalization, paranoia, and hallucinations (particularly visual and tactile types) (Medical Letter on Drugs and Therapeutics 1981; Greenblatt and Shader 1973; Farley et al. 1979).
8. Antidepressants (such as tofranil) can produce the anticholinergic delirium described above (Medical Letter on Drugs and Therapeutics 1981).

9. Over-the-counter sleep preparations (such as Sominex, Nytol, Sleepeze) contain scopolamine, which can induce anticholinergic delirium, tachycardia, and arrhythmia (Hooper et al. 1979).
10. Corticosteroids can induce hallucinations, especially after changes in dosage (Silber et al. 1984).
11. Actifed (triprolidine and pseudoephedrine) even in small or single doses can be followed by visual hallucinations for periods of up to four months (Spankey et al. 1984).
12. Phenergan (promethazine) cream has been reported to induce visual hallucations and agitation that has been attributed to anticholinergic action or inhibition of neurotransmitters (Shawn and McGuigan 1984).
13. Cimetidine in usual doses can cause visual hallucinations possibly due to the effect on brain receptors (Papp and Curtis 1984).
14. Procaine penicillin injections have been associated with anxiety hallucinations and seizures, probably the result of sudden elevations of serum procaine on the central nervous system (Silber and D'Angelo 1985).

Drug withdrawal hallucinations and delirium, although more common in adults, can occur in children who suddenly stop taking higher doses of barbiturates and diazepam (Valium) (Medical Letter on Drugs and Therapeutics 1981). Hallucinations secondary to withdrawal initially present as voices speaking in the third person, followed by signs of disorientation and later by visual and tactile hallucinations (Farley et al. 1979).

Sherwin and Mead (1975) reported on a nine-year-old American Indian boy who was brought to the emergency room because of hallucinations. The boy had a temperature of 101 degrees and a coarse tremor and was sweating profusely. He talked about seeing "big beetles" and experienced crawling sensations on his skin. The child was disoriented and confused. The father of the boy was a chronic alcoholic and apparently was unaware that his son was drinking some of the wine he had stored for his binges. A diagnosis of delirium tremens was consistent with the presenting symptoms.

Toxins and poisons—for example, jimson weed (atropine; Weiner 1961) and mercury (Maghazaji 1974)—can also have hallucinogenic and delirious effects. Recently, organic solvent abuse has been reported to be associated with unformed visual hallucinations long after the cessation of solvent inhalation (Channer and Stanley 1983). These effects are speculated to result from the high lipid solubility of the solvents. Organic lead compounds in gasoline also have high lipid solubility; there is a report of encephalopathy in a 15-year-old boy manifested by hallucinations, euphoria, ataxia, tremor, myoclonic movements, and choreiform motor movements following a history of gasoline sniffing (Goldings and Stewart 1982).

Toxic Hallucinosis Without Delirium

Drugs that induce hallucinations without delirium include amphetamines, methylphenidate (Medical Letter on Drugs and Therapeutics 1981), mescaline (Weiner 1961), psilocybin, LSD (lysergic acid diethylamide), marijuana (Lewis 1982), cocaine, and PCP (phencyclidine). Marijuana or tetrahydrocannabinol (THC) inhalation is manifested by illusions, euphoria, and rapid speech, but if taken in high doses, depersonalization, body image perceptual distortions, and visual hallucinations are not uncommon (Kaplan and Sadock 1981; Nystrom et al. 1979; West 1975). Average doses of LSD, however, results in marked distortion of body image, depersonalization experiences, mood fluctuations, and heightened perceptual activity with psychedelic embellishments, such as rainbow auras (Kaplan and Sadock 1981; Nystrom et al. 1979). Other amphetamine- and LSD-like hallucinogens are MDA (methylene dioxyamphetmine), STP (2,5-dimethoxy-4-methylamphetamine), DET (diethyltryptamine), DMT (dimethyltryptamine), mescaline, and psilocybin. Usually LSD produces a pseudohallucination in that the individual is aware that what he or she is seeing or hearing is not based on external reality. However, after PCP intoxication, thought blocking and disorganization similar to schizophrenia are differentiating aspects (Farley et al. 1979). Flashback experiences are particularly common after LSD ingestion. These experiences occur long after the acute effects have ceased, and the images may be of people, places, or objects. The flashback is probably related to state-dependent recall rather than to a hallucinatory experience (Siegel and Jarvik 1975). Both amphetamines and LSD are capable of causing paranoid psychotic states with primarily auditory hallucinations (Nystrom et al. 1979).

Cocaine is used for its euphoric effects, but severe effects such as tactile hallucinations and delusions and a paranoid psychosis make it a potentially dangerous drug (Kaplan and Sadock 1981).

Organic Brain Disorders Without Changes in Mental Status

Some organic brain disorders are manifested by hallucinations without any other changes in mental status. This is particularly true of certain types of brain tumors (Weiner 1961). Tumors of the temporal lobe typically are manifested by formed visual, olfactory, or gustatory hallucinations whereas tumors of the occipital lobe are manifested by unformed visual hallucinations such as flashes of light or color (Vick 1976). Auditory hallucinations described as ringing bells, escape of steam, or blowing of a whistle may be a rare effect of temporal lobe tumors (Vick 1976). Tumors compressing the optic nerves and optic chiasma have also caused simple and complex visual hallucinations (Weinberger and Grant 1940).

Epilepsy

Perceptual distortions and hallucinations have been described in some cases of temporal lobe epilepsy. The usual psychic aspects of temporal lobe epilepsy include déjà vu experiences, perceptual illusions, sudden change of emotional tone to fear or dread, aphasia or forced thinking, and automatic repetitive behaviors such as lip smacking (Laufer and Shetty 1979). As a rule the seizure episode rarely lasts more than two minutes. The individual usually recognizes the perceptions as ego-alien. Characteristically, the alien behavior, perception, or mood is abrupt and cannot be avoided. In addition there may be partial loss of consciousness, amnesia, and periods of confusion during postictal states.

Visual sensations of light, darkness, or color are more frequent than the complex dream-like experiences that are stereotypic flashbacks and give the feeling of reliving the past (Schmidt and Wilder 1968). Auditory and tactile hallucinations are less frequent. The content can be pleasant or unpleasant, such as foul smells or tastes, and the content is closely related to wishes and anxieties. The hallucination can occur as part of an aura or seizure discharge (especially during focal seizures; Weiner 1961).

A focal type of epilepsy called hallucinatory epilepsy has been described by Mulder et al. (1957). Hallucinations are brief, irresistible, paroxysmal, and stereotypic and are followed by a partial impairment of cerebral functioning. During the seizure there is a march of symptoms in which each component of the hallucination follows the next component in stereotypic fashion.

Occipital lobe epilepsy occurring in three children was described by Gastaut and Zifkin (1984). Each of the children experienced visual hallucinations of numbers followed by a brief loss of vision during the ictal phase.

Migraine Headache

Migraine headaches are often preceded by visual auras such as scintillating scotomata and complex visual experiences. Usually the hallucinations involve geometric designs or mosaics, but complex visual scenes are also possible (Weiner 1961). A sense that the body is growing smaller or bigger or changing in shape is not uncommon (Golden 1979). Some of Lewis Carroll's descriptions in *Alice in Wonderland* may have reflected the author's actual experiences as a migraine sufferer. Other symptoms of migraine headaches include aphasia, apraxia, déjà vu sensations, and trance-like states. Hachinski et al. (1973) reported that 77 percent of 100 children with migraines had binocular visual impairment, scotoma, vertigo, and ataxia, and 16 percent experienced visual hallucinations, micropsia, or macropsia.

Sleep Disorders

One of the primary symptoms in narcolepsy is the occurrence of hypnogogic hallucinations in association with sleep paralysis. The hallucinations are dream-like and have auditory and visual aspects of terrifying proportions (Ablon and Mack 1979; Wittig et al. 1983). Usually the hallucinations occur during the transition from waking to rapid eye movement (REM) sleep within minutes after falling asleep. Individuals are not aware of the unreality of the hallucination. At times they may simultaneously be in two worlds, for example, reporting dream-like experiences while responding to questions from an observer. Other symptoms of narcolepsy are sudden irresistible sleep attacks after meals or during monotonous situations and cataplexy (loss of muscle tone) after emotional events such as laughing.

Night terrors occur in very young children and are sometimes associated with sleepwalking and bedwetting. The child appears to be awake but actually cannot be reasoned with during the episode because he or she is in transition from Stage 3 or 4 sleep (Ablon and Mack 1979). To an observer the child is extremely anxious about a rather fragmented visual hallucination. The affected child remains agitated for about 10 minutes but has amnesia for the event, in contrast to nightmares, which are remembered and do not cause extreme anxiety.

Sleep Deprivation

Subjects who have been deprived of sleep for prolonged periods of time experience hallucinations, illusions, and disorientation. Mullaney et al. (1983) tested volunteer college students on continuous performance tasks (computer related) during a 42-hour period. Those subjects who were not allowed to sleep or nap had the poorest performance, and 30 percent experienced hallucinations. The subjects who were allowed six periodic naps of 1 hour performed better, but 20 percent also experienced hallucinations. Subjects who were allowed a 6-hour rest after 18 hours of work performed the best of all, and none experienced hallucinations.

Although no experiments have been conducted with children, sleep deprivation may be a potential cause of hallucinations.

Sensory Deprivation

Sensory deprivation may create panic and hallucinations (Weiner 1961). These symptoms pass if the person returns to his or her normal environment. As an example, life islands and laminar flow units are used to reduce bacterial infections during periods of drug- or disease-induced granulocytopenia that occurs in leukemia patients. Kellerman et al. (1977) reported on a survey of the directors of such units. Hallucinations were the fourth leading symptom, reported by 38.5% of the directors. The hallucinations were usually of slight intensity and involved all sensory modalities. Other symptoms reported to occur in patients undergoing isolation were anxiety, depression, withdrawal, disorientation, and irregular sleep. Children seemed to adjust to these units better than adults, and no child had to be removed for psychological reasons.

In an experiment by Davis et al. (1961), volunteers were exposed to a type of sensory deprivation by being placed in tank-type respirators surrounded by cubicles in a semidark room. The sensory deprivation was modified by allowing the subject to talk with a second person, who was also in a respirator in an adjacent cubicle. One group composed of pairs of strangers had 9 of 10 persons complete the 10½-hour experiment, but 6 of these subjects experienced hallucinations that were not as severe as the hallucinations of subjects without social contact. In another experiment (Goldberger and Holt 1958), which studied social isolation without sensory deprivation, no changes in thinking and no hallucinations were noted. The results of these experiments were similar to the responses of polio (Mendelson et al. 1958) and neurological (Leidermann et al. 1958) patients who required respirators as well as patients who had bilateral eye patches for periods of time (Weisman and Hackett 1958; Ziskind et al. 1960).

Acquired blindness secondary to cataract, optic nerve tumor, or retinal hemorrhage is a form of sensory deprivation that is quite prone to producing visual hallucinations (Weiner 1961). In contrast, the congenitally blind child does not have visual hallucinations. Similarly, amputations are types of sensory deprivation. Phantom limb phenomena occur for a period of time following surgery and gradually diminish as the sensory input from the stump increases (Weiner 1961). Such experiences do not occur if the child is born without a limb.

Hallucinations as Dissociative Symptoms

According to the *Diagnostic and Statistical Manual of Mental Disorders (Third Edition) (DSM-III;* American Psychiatric Association 1980), dissociative disorders involve sudden, temporary alterations in normally integrative functions of consciousness, identity, or motor behavior. Prominent symptoms are amnesia, fugue states, and depersonalization experiences. According to the Group for the Advancement of Psychiatry (1966), psychoneurotic disorder of the dissociative type is based on neurotic conflicts concerning repressed impulse or affect that result in temporary personality disorganization. The symptoms seem to be a defense against underlying anxiety. Supposedly these disorders are more common in persons having hysterical personality traits. Dissociative phenomena have similarities to conversion and hypnotic phenomena. West (1975) described dissociation in terms of information processing; that is, the central nervous system simultaneously and continuously scans and screens incoming information, processes old and new information, associates new information with old information, and controls behavioral responses. Breakdown or disturbance of the integrative functioning can result in clinical manifestations of dissociation.

Even though children rarely will be diagnosed as having a dissociative disorder, the concept of the dissociative defense mechanism is useful in explaining the phenomenon of hallucinations in nonpsychotic children without evidence of organicity. If hallucinations are viewed as alterations in the integrative aspects of consciousness, there is no doubt that they represent dissociative mental mechanisms. Dissociative symptoms involving hallucinations are likely to occur if the child is endowed with a vivid fantasy life and has a fundamental belief attributing value to hearing voices or seeing spirits.

The so-called neurotic hallucinatory experience in a child is usually an isolated perceptual experience that is somewhat repetitive in the same child (Kessler 1966). The child experiences a vivid sensation but knows others do not share the same experience. Usually there is no further cognitive elaboration regarding the experience (Kessler 1966). The most common type of hallucination is visual, especially scenes in which a phobia appears to come true (for example, the feared snakes, devil, or monsters become quite real; Kessler 1972). The psychodynamics of phobias such as the mechanisms of repression, displacement, and projection are also present in the dissociative hallucination. However, the hallucination goes one step further in concretization by putting distance between the self and the source of conflict (Kessler 1972). Another way of conceptualizing the dissociative hallucination is to consider it as regression to an earlier stage of ego functioning in which thought is equivalent to real image (Rothstein 1981).

McKegney (1967) viewed some hallucinations as conversion symptoms representing a revival of experiences that occurred in the past at the time of satisfying relationships. Most of the time a psychological stress precipitates the hallucination. Proctor's (1958) original idea that excessive stimulation combined with a punitive moralism as a breeding ground for hysterical symptoms probably holds true for some cases of hallucinations. Esman (1962) noted that visual exposure to sexual acts in puritanical families was a factor in his case reports. Adolescents may be particularly vulnerable to dissociative phenomena because of increased sexual desires, high suggestibility, emotional lability, and striving for mastery of identity issues (Kessler 1972).

Pseudopsychosis is a term now used to describe the so-called hysterical psychosis. The predominant symptoms are delusions or hallucinations, absence of thought or mood disorder, absence of organic brain syndrome or medical problems, and a close association between symptoms and psychological factors (for example, symptoms help the individual avoid an activity or get support from the environment; Bishop and Holt 1980). The literature mostly reports adult cases, but Bishop and Holt (1980) described a 12-year-old girl with phobias and hysterical personality traits.

Hallucinations in Reaction to Stress

Severe stress is associated with overwhelming anxiety and/or depression. The young child may attempt to deal with the emotional stimuli by using various defense mechanisms such as repression, projection, and displacement (Lewis 1979). These defense mechanisms can be incorporated into more elaborate phobias and dissociative–conversion phenomena described previously. The child may attempt to deal with the stress in terms of previously learned patterns of behavior. Thus, the child might abandon abstract conceptualizations and translate the problems into concrete perceptions (perhaps hallucinations) by which he or she can organize to act and establish equilibrium (Weiner 1961; Lukianowicz, 1969; Aug and Ables, 1971). A child with severe anxiety disorder and fear of the dark may report staring eyes or glaring mythical animals.

Lukianowicz (1969) discussed the case history of a nine-year-old girl who became afraid to go upstairs to her bathroom. She apparently heard voices telling her that her mother would leave when she went upstairs. In the dark she also experienced visual hallucinations of dead people and crashed cars. The mother was an anxious and depressed middle-aged lady who had been hospitalized frequently. The father had chronic bronchitis and showed no interest in the child. Both parents quarreled in front of her. Psychodynamic aspects of this case included an anxious mother projecting her own fears onto the child, separation anxiety in the child, fearfulness in the child related to the parental arguments, anxiety in the girl related to a recent move to a new neighborhood and new school, and an unhappy memory of an automobile accident the year previously in which the child and her father were injured. The hallucinations were clearly related to the anxiety state in the child as a result of an accumulation of life stresses and frightening events.

Posttraumatic stress disorder (PTSD) is often associated with repetitive nightmares, vivid imagination, and related illusions in an attempt to cope with the previous trauma in a more masterful way. Hallucinations are possible symptoms in PTSD, but it is more usual to have repetitive intrusive intense images of the past traumatic event even after situations that might be objectively assessed as mildly stressful. Horowitz (1975) considered this type of repetitive compulsion to be adaptationally important. She regarded the images to be an "active memory" for the purpose of completing cognitive assimilation and accommodation. The cognitive appraisal may take a long time and may not match with the person's "ideal image." Intolerable emotions such as guilt or shame may keep the memory active so that an intrusive quality to the images may assume hallucinatory proportions if there are shifts in the normal repressive defense mechanisms (Horowitz 1975).

Children have reportedly experienced PTSD following catastrophic situations (Frederick 1984). Some children who witnessed horrifying events, such as the death of another, have had hallucinations of ghosts of the departed (Terr 1984). Intense perceptual experiences and intrusive images have been reported in children who have witnessed violence such as rape, homicide, and suicide (Pynoos 1984).

The various reports in the literature of hallucinations in young children usually involve stress situations that are more ordinary. The stress can be specifically related to developmental issues (Aug and Ables 1971) or family crises (Aug and Ables 1971; Esman 1962). Lewis (1979) believed that adolescents had to be exposed to overwhelming stress before hallucinations would occur.

Hallucinations Related to Cultural and Family Factors

Hallucinations have reportedly been more frequent in deprived low-income families (Wilking and Paoli 1966). However, Rothstein (1981) pointed out that poverty included a constellation of many factors, such as emotional deprivation, overstimulation, neglect, and modes of impulse and fantasy expression that might affect the manifestation of hallucinations. Bender and Lipkowitz

(1940) observed hallucinations to be more frequent in black children and speculated that this was due to a richer fantasy life and
greater exposure to stress. However, most of the blacks in these
studies were from the lower social classes, which most likely was
the dominant factor. Emotional deprivation, also prominent in
lower class children, may cause the children to substitute gratifications to make up for the harsh realities of life.

Bender and Lipkowitz (1940) gave a case history of Viola, a nine-
year-old black girl with an IQ of 91. The father had deserted the
family but periodically returned to demand money from the
mother to support his drinking. There were six children. The
mother was poverty stricken and too preoccupied with meeting
the physical needs of her children to worry about showing affection.

Viola had a history of staying out on the streets all night and
hiding under her stoop. She did this to avoid ugly scenes with the
father and to escape punishment. She developed a vivid fantasy
life that included daydreams of a bogeyman and a giant chasing
her and of becoming a witch with special powers. Auditory hallucinations consisted of voices of tiny ladies either threatening her,
entertaining her, or telling her to go home. This case demonstrated the role of the superego as well as substitution mechanisms
in hallucinations.

In some situations hallucinations are fostered by superstitious
parents or parents with deviant religious and/or mystical beliefs
(Lewis 1979). The child uses hallucinations as a means to get
attention from the parents. In the case history (Bender and
Lipkowitz 1940) of Oscar, a nine-year-old boy who had auditory
and visual hallucinations, the parents thought that Oscar had a
special gift and tended to encourage the hallucinations. He reported seeing lions on the street and hearing voices like spirits
calling his name. These hallucinatory experiences were simple
and did not demonstrate special emotional mechanisms other
than seeking extra attention from the parents.

Some case reports of hallucinations mention fundamentalist
religious beliefs, which were speculated to stimulate hallucinations involving the conflict between good and evil (Aug and Ables

1971; Strauss 1969). Other religious practices such as speaking in tongues or seeing visions can provide role models for children to imitate (Aug and Ables 1971).

A special type of cultural influence occurs when there is a belief in evil spirits or ghosts or other supernatural creatures that is supported by periodic sightings of such spirits by individuals within the culture. A study of 12 Colombian (South America) families who had seen the demon *"el duende"* was conducted in 1975 by Carlos Leon. The *el duende* spirit was described as a pot-bellied, dark-complexioned male who wore a large hat and was an expert horseman. His actions were generally described as destructive (for example, hitting or hurting people), mischievous, erotic, or humorous. In Leon's study many family members had experienced the influence of the spirit. There were only 13 key persons (those mainly involved with the spirit), and of those, 4 were between 10 and 19 years of age. Psychological symptoms of these key persons included auditory and visual hallucinations, anxiety, insomnia, trance-like states, and suicidal impulses. Leon thought that 4 of the key persons had epilepsy. Other diagnoses were dissociative hysteria (5 people), chronic anxiety and depression (3 people), and schizophrenia (1 person). In this study the interaction of culture, folklore, faulty learning, and impaired brain functioning were important dimensions.

Hallucinations Related to Personality Disorder

The schizotypal personality is basically an adult borderline personality disorder, but it can occur during adolescence (American Psychiatric Association 1980). The symptoms of this condition include speech oddities, magical thinking, and bizarre fantasies, but not loose thought association. At times of stress, a brief reactive psychosis is possible, and during this episode hallucinations may be present. Childers (1931) reported a 16-percent incidence of hallucinations in 148 schizoid children.

Although the borderline child is not an official *DSM-III* diagnosis, Morton Chetnik (1979) described such an entity and stated that it is characterized by delusions and hallucinations. According to Chetnik (1979), these children project their own aggressive impulses and view the outside world as a frightening place. The children are very anxious (fearing separation from their parents). They remain in contact with reality but reality testing is distorted. Other symptoms are social withdrawal, obsessive thinking, and compulsive rituals.

Hallucinations Related to Psychotic Disorders

For a discussion of hallucinations in children suffering from psychotic disorders, the reader is referred to Chapter 3.

Case History 1: Dynamic Aspects of Hallucinations in an Eight-Year-Old

Ann was an 8-year-old child, the second of three children, who was referred for evaluation because she reported to her mother that she had seen an angel and a devil at school and they had talked to her about winning and losing a race (during a physical education class). The devil told her to win the race while the angel told her it did not matter whether she won or lost. In actuality she lost the race and used the hallucination as an excuse for losing the race. The child was a good athlete and took pride in her skills. However, she thought her parents wanted her to win. At other times the devil's, angel's, and her mother's voices argued inside her head, causing her to cry out in an attempt to get rid of them. She did know that other children did not have similar hallucinations.

At night Ann had occasional nightmares in which a witch chased her and threatened to kill her. The witch was described as fat, wearing tattered clothes, and having black hair and a face just like her mother's. These repetitive dreams no doubt were stimulated by conflict between mother and child.

The mother was a narcissistic lady who worked as a legal secretary and was respected for her ability. She complained frequently about back pain and sought relief from several doctors who could do little to help her. She was very controlling and critical with her husband and children. There were frequent arguments and physical fights between the mother and father. At times the father would beat the girl to satisfy his wife. Eventually the father withdrew more from family life and made no attempt to give emotional support to his daughter.

The mother stated that Ann had been a problem since birth. She was a "blue baby" and had to be in an incubator for two days. Then she was diagnosed as having genu varum, which required braces. Ann "cried all the time," and her mother could not nurse or appease her. During these early years Ann's mother felt quite frustrated because her husband was overseas. Other developmental problems that irritated the mother were Ann's bedwetting until age six years and encopresis until age seven years and articulation problems until age seven. In addition she was quite worried about what she called Ann's "chronic masturbation."

The mother had brought Ann to mental health clinics on several occasions for alleged "hyperactivity," and on one occasion the child was treated with ritalin. She could not tolerate Ann's attitudes. She said the child had a "supercilious smile" and a "clenched jaw" and enjoyed embarrassing her in public situations; for example, she clearly remembered the time when Ann commented in a restaurant about the scar on her face. Ann's mother attributed evil intentions to much of her daughter's routine behaviors and regarded the child's school misconduct and bedwetting as deliberate attempts to aggravate her.

One of Ann's mother's biggest complaints concerned the inadequacy of previous doctors, therapists, and teachers. She was particularly angry at the school for not recognizing her daughter as a gifted child, and she demanded that Ann be placed in the gifted program. After much harassment the school did place Ann in their gifted program (despite a full scale IQ of about 100).

Ann enjoyed relating to peers and teachers at school. She did poorly in the gifted program and desired to be placed in the regular program. No one at school reported odd or unusual behaviors, but teachers did think that Ann was in need of a great deal of love and affection, which they tried to provide.

During the evaluation interview, Ann spoke spontaneously about her dislike for her mother's not showing any interest in her. However, she wished to please her mother and wished that her mother could like her sometime. When lonely or under stress, she coped by talking or singing to herself. She spoke freely about the auditory and visual hallucinations and described the experiences as if they were occurring outside of herself. Her self-concept was generally poor, but she enjoyed the attention she received from her teachers. She did experience stress from demands put on her in the gifted program.

A *DSM-III* diagnosis of adjustment disorder, with mixed disturbances of emotions and conduct, was made. The stresses in this girl's life included her mother's expectation that she be gifted when in fact she was no more than average in ability, the long-standing parental marital problems, the mother's overt rejection, and scapegoating by all family members. The mother's psycho-pathology was quite marked, and her ideas concerning Ann were of delusional proportions. She was unable to view Ann as a person of value in her own right but tended to regard her as an extension of herself (gifted child) or as having powers of a person possessed with an evil spirit. The hallucinations were interpreted by the mother as a sign that her daughter must be truly crazy. From the child's point of view, the hallucinations were much like real life conflicts with her mother. The commands of the devil were similar to mother expectations. Ann tried to follow the directions of the good angel, which could be interpreted as a personification of her superego. The hallucinations were not helpful in establish-ing a *DSM-III* diagnosis, but they did offer important information about the dynamics of the relationship between mother and daughter.

Case History 2: Hallucinations Secondary to Drug Abuse

Stefanie was a 17-year-old white female admitted to the adolescent ward of a state hospital because of persistent hallucinations. She heard voices outside her head telling her not to smoke and not to wear certain clothing, but she never experienced visual hallucinations. She was aware that the hallucinations were not real, but she did experi-ence anxiety and shakiness. Her thinking was otherwise logical, with no evidence of loose thought associations or delusions. The affect was somewhat constricted.

This girl's past history revealed extensive conduct problems since age 10 years. She had stolen frequently and run away from home and was subsequently placed in numerous foster homes. Eventually she started taking illegal drugs. At age 15 years she ran away to Mexico and lived with a gang whose main activities included stealing and drug running. During this period she used LSD, PCP, amphetamines, and heroin, and she smoked marijuana on a daily basis. The girl voluntarily left the gang and returned to the United States to seek help for drug abuse. Prior to her hospitalization she sniffed paint on a regular basis. Hallucinations began about five months prior to admis-sion.

Psychiatric diagnoses included conduct disorder and mixed drug abuse. The auditory hallucinations seemed to be directly related to the effects of various hallucinatory drugs on the brain. The description of the hallucination was very similar to the pseudo-hallucinations experienced after LSD ingestion. There was some evidence that the patient experienced flashbacks because the perceptions occurred months after drug ingestion had ceased. It is also noteworthy that the voices took on the character of a helping person trying to correct the girl's previous misbehaviors.

Case History 3: Hallucinations Related to Depression and Grief

A 12-year-old girl experienced increased anxiety after starting junior high school three months prior to her admission to a psychiatric hospital. The lack of structure in an open classroom setting, different school routines, and increased number of students threatened the girl's security. She gradually became depressed and began to hallucinate that a human voice was telling her to take aspirin to kill herself. She tried to kill herself by overdosing.

Past history revealed that her stepfather had died suddenly two years previously and that she had never resolved her grief over his death. On occasions she had frightening dreams about her stepfather. Two additional stresses were the mother's remarriage to a man the patient resented and the mother's conversion to the Jehovah's Witness religion, the practice of which was hard on family members.

The hallucination was interpreted as a phenomenon of depression, which resulted from cumulative stresses and unresolved grief. This depression was not regarded as psychotic but rather as an emotional disturbance secondary to an adjustment disorder.

Case History 4: Hallucinations Associated With Dissociative Experiences

A 16-year-old Mexican-American male was brought to the emergency room because of suicidal thoughts that were communicated to students at his school. He was admitted to the psychiatric service. He reported that he felt depressed and became upset at school when some boys called him weird and a girl gave him "the cold shoulder." While other students watched, he screamed, put his fist against the wall, and voiced a suicidal desire. He then ran out of the school building, felt dazed, and wandered to an isolated location. During this time he heard the voice of his dead aunt calling him to join her in a peaceful place. When other students found him, he gave no response to them and seemed to have little memory for what happened.

The boy was reared by his great aunt, who had died four years prior to his admission. After her death he had lived with his natural father (who was divorced from his mother) for about three years. He felt that his father did not want him and then went to live with his natural mother and four siblings. He again experienced feelings of rejection as a result of his siblings' teasing and mother's criticizing him and comparing him to his brother. In high school he had difficulty in his special education program.

Life with the great aunt had been quite comfortable because he was well taken care of and had no siblings to compete with. His aunt doted on him and even told him that if she died his mother would not take good care of him. The aunt was of American Indian and Mexican descent, and she believed in magic spells and devils. She told him that bad things would happen to people who got too close to him.

When he came to live with his mother, he had to share a one-bedroom house with five other persons and felt pressure because he had no space for himself. He began to fantasize, take long walks by himself, and romanticize about his past life with the great aunt. In addition he became obsessed with the martial arts, and his peers began to criticize him. He would hold in his angry and sad feelings because he had no friends with whom he felt comfortable.

On admission the boy seemed mildly depressed but denied suicide attempts or intentions and also denied sleep and appetite problems. There was no history of drug abuse or experimentation. He stated that at times he heard the voice of the dead aunt in his head. This would usually occur when he felt stressed, at which time he preferred to go off to be by himself. The Minnesota Multiphasic Personality Inventory (MMPI) (Dahlstrom et al. 1972) results indicated that this was a boy who experienced social isolation but desired to have friends. He tended to present a more pathological picture of himself. However, he did experience ideas of external influence, such as the devil's casting spells. This seemed more related to the influence of the great aunt.

This patient was diagnosed as having adjustment disorder with disturbance of emotions and an atypical dissociative disorder with trance-like states and auditory hallucinations. The hallucinations were ego-alien phenomena but also comforting at times of stress. The aunt's belief in spirits and devils may have influenced the hallucinatory and dissociative behaviors.

Case History 5: Hallucinations Associated With Personality Disorder

A 13-year-old male was admitted to an adolescent psychiatric unit following a suicide threat and strange behaviors at home. His adoptive parents were concerned because they found him wandering in the house in the middle of the night and staring over them while they slept. The boy claimed he was upset following a whipping by the father, who had smashed his radio because he listened to rock music. He felt he could do nothing right in his home and wanted to have a new set of parents. Ego-alien voices told him to kill his parents and to find new parents. He felt the voices were telling him to do "wrong things" and at times felt that the voices could control his will. The year prior to his admission he put an aspirin compound (Anacin) in his parents' milk, but they did not suffer any ill effects. The parents were worried about the most recent incident because a butcher knife was missing. However, no attempt was made on their lives, and the child denied any such intention.

A mental status examination revealed no current hallucinations, no loose associations, normal orientation, flat affect, suspiciousness regarding parents, denial of anger or depression, and normal sleep and eating patterns. He did admit to previous auditory hallucinations that directed him to leave his parents and on one occasion to kill them. On the ward the boy did seek out the approval of the staff and was able to relate positively to one or two peers.

This child had been neglected during the first six years of his life. At age seven he was adopted by a family who frequently took in foster children. Over the years he resented the attention given to the many foster children who stayed briefly in the home. In addition he felt stress because peers teased him at school for not being smart. There had never been any previous conduct problems. In fact, the child had rigid attitudes toward good and evil. He often prayed to God for help but never had hallucinations involving God. Because he had difficulty tolerating angry feelings, he generally denied these feelings or experienced the feelings as ego-alien voices.

A diagnosis of schizotypal personality disorder was made. The patient was generally a loner, maintained a constricted affect, was suspicious about the motives of others, and was sensitive to criticism. His thinking was somewhat odd in that he thought he could get rid of his adoptive parents and find a new set of parents, much as one would buy something at the store. Reality testing was poor, and his problem solving was rather concrete and simplistic. Under the stress of the many foster children at home, the boy experienced angry feelings, which he could not tolerate. These angry feelings became transformed into ego-alien voices directing him to kill his parents. At such times he was probably in a psychotic state, but he quickly reconstituted to his more usual schizotypal personality.

DISCUSSION

Hallucinations can occur in most diagnostic categories and therefore have limited value in providing answers to diagnostic questions. The symptom is nonspecific but can provide more useful information regarding psychodynamics, defenses, and impulses.

The aims or rationale for particular types of hallucinations are often not in the awareness of the person hallucinating but readily discernible to the professional who does a detailed history and mental status examination. Hallucinations are often a way to modify harsh realities, an escape mechanism. Closely related to escape is the hallucination that satisfies wishes and fantasies, such as the desire for pleasure or enhanced self-esteem. Most children do not tolerate extreme feelings of fear and/or anxiety. The hallucination is a way of projecting anxiety to an external, concrete source. In addition, their distress is obvious to others who might relieve their distress. In a similar manner, hostility can be defended against by projecting it to an outside object. Some hallucinations help to relieve or expiate guilt. A common aim of hallucinations is to relive a past traumatic event, such as the death of a relative, or even past happy events. Old relationships are thereby maintained as the child attempts to recreate or correct his or her past, gaining a feeling of mastery.

Rothstein (1981) has classified the psychodynamic functions of hallucinations according to Freud's structural concepts. Many of these functions overlap with the aims and purposes of hallucinations discussed previously. Thus, hallucinations can be expressions or projections of id drives, such as the aggressive and sexual drives, and manifested by extreme fearfulness. Sometimes hallucinations can represent superego functions for the purpose of impulse control. The content would be scoldings or warnings about dangers and unacceptable impulses. Finally, hallucinations can be expressions of ego functions; for example, efforts to recall repressed memories, attempts to master or deal with losses, wish-fulfillment expressions, attempts to displace unacceptable impulses, and manifestations of confused inner or outer reality.

In considering the diagnostic significance of hallucinations, Rothstein (1981) stressed the developmental perspective. He listed the importance of each of the following factors in making a diagnostic assessment:

1. The child's age—In general, the older child who hallucinates will have a more severe prognosis.
2. The child's developmental progress—Lags in development and intellectual functioning may limit the child's ability to differentiate reality from subjective imagery.
3. The child's general level of functioning, especially emotional, social, and behavioral—Hallucinations occurring in the absence of satisfying relationships are less ominous than their occurrence despite emotionally satisfying relationships.
4. The degree of consciousness at the time of the hallucination— The occurrence of hallucinations in twilight states is less significant than their occurrence in full consciousness.
5. The ease with which the child gains awareness that the hallucination is not real—A clear awareness concerning the unreality of the hallucination would indicate a less severe disorder.
6. The ease with which the hallucination is modified or ceases to occur is associated with a favorable prognosis.
7. The degree of the hallucination dissonance with real-world objects would most likely point toward a psychiatric type of disorder.

References

Ablon SL, Mack JE: Sleep disorders, in Basic Handbook of Child Psychiatry, vol 2. Edited by Noshpitz J. New York, Basic Books, 1979, 643–660

Allen T, Agus B: Hyperventilation leading to hallucinations. Am J Psychiatry 125:632-637, 1968

American Psychiatric Association: Diagnostic and Statistical Manual of Mental Disorders (Third Edition). Washington, DC, American Psychiatric Association, 1980

Aug R, Ables B: Hallucinations in nonpsychotic children. Child Psychiatry Hum Dev 1:152-167, 1971

Bender L, Lipkowitz H: Hallucinations in children. Am J Orthopsychiatry 10:471-490, 1940

Bishop E, Holt AR: Pseudopsychosis: a reexamination of the concepts of hysterical psychosis. Compr Psychiatry 21:150-161, 1980

Channer KS, Stanley S: Persistent visual hallucinations secondary to chronic solvent encephalopaty: case report and review of the literature. J Neurol Neurosurg Psychiatry 46:83-86, 1983

Chetnik M: The borderline child, in Basic Handbook of Child Psychiatry, vol 2. Edited by Noshpitz J. New York, Basic Books, 1979, 304-321

Childers AT: The study of some schizoid children. Journal of Mental Hygiene 15:106-134, 1931

Connell M: Psychiatric emergencies in childhood. Aust Fam Physician [Suppl] 6:5-9, 1977

Cunningham B, McKinney P: Patient acceptance of dissociative anesthetics. Plast Reconstr Surg 72:22-26, 1983

Dahlstrom W, Welsh G, Dahlstrom L: An MMPI Handbook. Volume 1: Clinical Interpretation. Minneapolis, University of Minnesota Press, 1972

Davis J, McCourt W, Courtney J, et al: Sensory deprivation: the role of social isolation. Arch Gen Psychiatry 5:84-90, 1961

Despert JL: Delusional and hallucinatory experiences in children. Am J Psychiatry 104:528-537, 1948

Drugs that cause psychiatric symptoms. Med Lett Drugs Ther 23(3):9–12, February 6, 1981

Esman A: Visual hallucinations in young children. Psychoanal Study Child 17:334–344, 1962

Farley G, Eckhardt L, Hebert F: Handbook of Child and Adolescent Psychiatric Emergencies. New York, Medical Examination Publishing Co, 1979

Frederick C: Children traumatized by catastrophical situations, in Syllabus and Scientific Proceedings, American Psychiatric Association 137th annual meeting. Washington, DC, American Psychiatric Association, 1984, 130–131

Frost E: Central nervous system effects of oxide, in Nitrous Oxide/N_2O. Edited by Eger E. New York, Elsevier, 1985, 157–176

Garralda M: Hallucinations in psychiatrically disordered children: preliminary communication. J R Soc Med 75:181–184, 1982

Gastaut H, Zifkin B: Ictal visual hallucinations of numerals. Neurology 34:950–953, 1984

Goldberger L, Holt R: Experimental interference with reality contact (perceptual isolation): method and group results. J Nerv Ment Dis 127:99–112, 1958

Golden G: The Alice in Wonderland syndrome in juvenile migraine. Pediatrics 63:517–519, 1979

Goldings A, Stewart R: Organic lead encephalopathy: behavioral change and movement disorder following gasoline inhalation. J Clin Psychiatry 43:70–72, 1982

Greenblatt D, Shader R: Drug therapy: anticholinergics. N Eng J Med 288:1215–1219, 1973

Group for the Advancement of Psychiatry: Psychopathological Disorders in Childhood: Theoretical Considerations and a Proposed Classification. New York, Committee on Child Psychiatry, Group for the Advancement of Psychiatry, 1966

Hachinski V, Porchawka J, Steele J: Visual symptoms in the migraine syndrome. Neurology 23:570–579, 1973

Hooper R, Conner C, Rumack B: Acute poisoning from over-the-counter sleep preparations. Journal of the American College of Emergency Physicians 8:98–100, 1979

Horowitz M: Hallucinations: an information processing approach, in Hallucinations. Edited by Siegel RK and West LJ. New York, Wiley, 1975, 163–195

Kaplan H, Sadock B: Modern Synopsis of the Comprehensive Textbook of Psychiatry, 3rd ed. Baltimore, Williams & Wilkins, 1981

Kellerman J, Rigler D, Siegel S: The psychological effect of isolation in protected environments. Am J Psychiatry 134:563–565, 1977

Kessler J: Psychoneurosis in children, in Psychopathology of Childhood. Englewood Cliffs, NJ, Prentice-Hall, 1966, 244

Kessler J: Neurosis in childhood, in Manual of Childhood Psychopathology. Edited by Wolman B. New York, McGraw-Hill, 1972, 387–435

Laufer M, Shetty T: Acute and chronic brain syndromes, in Basic Handbook of Child Psychiatry, vol 2. Edited by Noshpitz J. New York, Basic Books, 1979, 381–402

Leidermann P, Mendelson J, Wexler D: Sensory deprivation: clinical aspects. AMA Arch Intern Med 101:389–396, 1958

Leon C: "El duende" and other incubi: suggestive interactions between culture, the devil and the brain. Arch Gen Psychiatry 32:155–162, 1975

Levin M: Auditory hallucinations in nonpsychotic children. Am J Psychiatry 88:1119–1152, 1932

Lewis M: Differential diagnosis, in Basic Handbook of Child Psychiatry, vol 2. Edited by Noshpitz J. New York, Basic Books, 1979, 144–156

Lewis M: Clinical Aspects of Child Development, Philadelphia, Lee & Febiger, 1982

Lukianowicz N: Hallucination in nonpsychotic children. Psychiatr Clin (Basel) 2:321-337, 1969

Maghazaji H: Psychiatric aspects of methylmercury poisoning. J Neurol Neurosurg Psychiatry 37:954-958, 1974

McKegney F: Auditory hallucinations as a conversion symptom: a theoretical proposal with two case illustrations. Compr Psychiatry 8:80-89, 1967

Mendelson J, Solomon P, Lindemann E: Hallucinations of poliomyelitis patients during treatment in a respirator. J Nerv Ment Dis 126:421-428, 1958

Mulder D, Bickford R, Dodge H: Hallucinatory epilepsy: complex hallucinations as focal seizures. Am J Psychiatry 113:1100-1102, 1957

Mullaney D, Kripke D, Fleck P, et al: Sleep loss and nap effects on sustained continuous performance. Psychophysiology 20:643-650, 1983

Nystrom K, Bal A, Labrecque V: Substance abuse, in Basic Handbook of Child Psychiatry, vol 2. Edited by Noshpitz J. New York, Basic Books, 1979, 600-636

Papp KA, Curtis RM: Cimetidine-induced psychosis in a 14-year-old girl. Can Med Assoc J 131:1081-1084, 1984

Proctor JT: Hysteria in childhood. Am J Orthopsychiatry 28:394-407, 1958

Pynoos R: Children traumatized by witnessing violence, in Syllabus and Scientific Proceedings, American Psychiatric Association 137th annual meeting. Washington, DC, American Psychiatric Association, 1984, 130-131

Rothstein A: Hallucinatory phenomena in children: a critique of the literature. J Am Acad Child Psychiatry 20:623-635, 1981

Sankey RJ, Nunn AJ, Sills JA: Visual hallucinations in children receiving decongestants. Br Med J 288:1369, 1984

Schmidt RP, Wilder BJ: Epilepsy. Philadelphia, FA Davis Co, 1968

Sherwin D, Mead B: Delirium tremens in a nine year old child. Am J Psychiatry 132:1210–1212, 1975

Shawn DH, McGuigan MA: Poisoning from dermal absorption of promethazine. Can Med Assoc J 130:1460–1461, 1984

Silber T, Chatoor I, White P: Psychiatric manifestations of systemic lupus erythematosus in children and adolescents. A review. Clin Pediatr 23:331–335, 1984

Silber T, D'Angelo L: Psychosis and seizures following the injection of penicillen G procaine. Am J Dis Child 139:335–337, 1985

Siegel RK, Jarvik ME: Drug induced hallucinations in animals and man, in Hallucinations. Edited by Siegel RK and West LJ. New York, Wiley, 1975, 81–161

Simonds JF: Hallucinations in nonpsychotic children and adolescents. J of Youth and Adolescence 4:171–182, 1975

Strauss JS: Hallucinations and delusions as points on continua function. Arch Gen Psychiatry 21:581–586, 1969

Terr L: Children traumatized in small groups, in Syllabus and Scientific Proceedings, American Psychiatric Association 137th annual meeting, Washington, DC, American Psychiatric Association, 1984, 130–131

Vick N: Grinker's Neurology, 7th ed. Springfield, IL, Charles C Thomas, 1976, 401–402

Weinberger LM, Grant FC: Visual Hallucinations and their neuroptical correlates. Arch Ophthalmol 23:166–199, 1940

Weiner M: Hallucinations in children. Arch Gen Psychiatry 5:544–553, 1961

Weisman AD, Hackett TP: Psychosis after eye surgery. N Engl J Med 258:1284–1287, 1958

West LJ: A clinical and theoretical overview of hallucinatory phenomena, in Hallucinations. Edited by Siegel RK and West LJ. New York, Wiley, 1975, 287–311

Wilking V, Paoli C: The hallucinatory experience, J Am Acad Child Psychiatry 5:431–440, 1966

Wittig R, Zorick F, Roehrs T, et al: Narcolepsy in a seven year old child. J Pediatr 102:725–727, 1983

Ziskind E, Jones H, Filante W, et al: Observations on mental symptoms in eye patched patients: hypnagogic symptoms in sensory deprivation. Am J Psychiatry 116:893–900, 1960

Hallucinations in Psychotic and Depressed Children

William Chambers, M.D.

3

Hallucinations in Psychotic and Depressed Children

The diagnostic relevance of hallucinatory phenomena in children and in adolescents has been the subject of considerable discussion over the course of this century. The issue has generally lacked clarity and focus, in large measure because the issue has been tied closely to the issue of the diagnosis of psychosis and psychotic disorders in childhood and adolescence, and this has been a complex and uncertain discussion at best. As recently as 1963, the eminent Swedish child psychiatrist Anne-Lise Annell wrote

> It has . . . proved impossible to find a definition satisfying everybody for [psychosis in children]. No precise symptom or combination of symptoms exists which classifies a state of sickness as psychotic. The selection of the primary material [for her study] was consequently made by a subjective estimate of the symptoms. . . . the term psychosis or psychotic syndrome has been used in the broad sense; where a doubt existed whether a psychosis was present, the case was included in the material. (p 237)

Two primary issues relate to the diagnosis of psychotic disorders in children and adolescents: a) the fact of immature cognitive and social development in children and adolescents and its impact on manifestations and assessment of psychotic phenomena and b) the concept of "childhood schizophrenia" (American Psychiatric Association 1968) as a unitary disease entity encompassing most, if not all, of the psychotic disorders in childhood, depending on the classification scheme that was used or adhered to.

These two issues were extant before the advent of the *Diagnostic and Statistical Manual of Mental Disorders (Third Edition)* (*DSM-III*; American Psychiatric Association 1980) and its multiaxial diagnostic format and the clarity with which that format allows the issue to be addressed. The issues that led to the development of multiaxial diagnostic schemes in child psychiatry in 1972 (Rutter et al. 1973), and subsequently in the *DSM-III* (Williams 1985), were, I believe, in some good measure responsible for the lack of scientific progress in this area. Until axes reflecting syndromal diagnosis, cognitive developmental abnormalities, medical/neurological disorders, psychosocial influences and stress, and course were each considered separately, diagnosis of childhood psychoses was bound to be a confusing hodgepodge in which investigators gave one or more of these parameters greater diagnostic weight. The study of psychotic phenomena in children and adolescents was further hampered by the infrequent occurrence of psychotic disorders in children and adolescents, so that any one center required long periods to assemble a sample sufficiently large to study. Kolvin, for example, required about eight years to assemble a sample of 33 late-onset (nonautistic) psychotic children and adolescents for his study. In fact, the author is aware of only nine studies in the English-language literature since 1943 that purport to study nonautistic schizophrenic disorders in children and adolescents. Progress has thus been slow in the classification of psychotic children and adolescents. Such lack of diagnostic clarity has hampered research into the pathogenesis and treatment of childhood psychotic disorders.

In this chapter I will review the literature on hallucinations in children and adolescents from the perspective of *DSM-III* and the Rutter et al. (1973) multiaxial diagnostic scheme toward two purposes: a) to ascertain the current state of knowledge on diagnostic issues relating to hallucinations and psychotic disorders in children and adolescents and b) to identify areas requiring investigation. From this perspective, I will address the two issues elucidated, that is, the impact of children's cognitive and psychosocial immaturity on assessment and symptomatology and the diagnosis of childhood schizophrenia.

DEVELOPMENTAL ISSUES

Development of the Sense of Reality

Bleuler (1950) described the fantasy plan of children as a "normal" form of "autistic" thinking, one of his fundamental signs of schizophrenia. The issues as regard to childhood schizophrenia thus are as follows:

1. How is one to determine a pathological degree of impaired reality testing in a person for whom this capacity is developing at the age in question and in an age range where cognitive development occurs at different rates in different individuals?
2. Is it possible that children have a lower threshold to manifesting secondary or productive signs and symptoms of psychosis or schizophrenia, particularly hallucinations, and that such signs and symptoms have lesser or different psychopathological import when occurring in children than when occurring in adults?

Furthermore, children's cognitive immaturity could impact on the assessment process itself, as well as on the symptomatology.

The above issues concerning the impact of the developmental immaturity of children on the diagnosis of psychotic disorders have been the subject of remarkably little systematic research. I will review what has been learned and in the process will identify areas for future investigation.

Orientation Toward Consensual Reality

The assessment of hallucinations in children depends primarily on the report of the child, either to parents, teachers, or the examiner. In our study of psychotic symptoms reported by prepubertal children with major depressive disorder (Chambers et al. 1982), only a third of the parents were aware that the children experienced such hallucinations.

Several things are required for a child to accurately answer probes in an interview, for example, the experiences that the child reports (verbal symbols for the subjective experience) must mean the same thing to the examiner, who decodes these verbal symbols according to his or her own symbolic system. The examiner's diagnostic system is based on a consensus among adults that certain verbal designations of experience are equivalent between adults, even between psychotic adults and diagnosticians. The problem in assessing children is that the capacity to assume an attitude oriented toward consensual reality is developing, or incompletely developed, in the years up through adolescence. Before then, children are oriented, to varying degrees, toward an egocentric reality with idiosyncratic meanings and referents (Inhelder and Piaget 1958). Thus, one may not, when interviewing children, be as certain as one can be when interviewing adults that what is communicated and interpreted by the diagnostician represents what was experienced by the child. Although such difficulties exist in the diagnostic assessment of adults, the fact of children's cognitive immaturity in this area places an added burden on the diagnostician to verify the information he or she receives. Such verification is exceedingly difficult to acquire.

Language Development

Psychosis is a concept that experienced clinicians have difficulty defining (Annell 1963) and that has its roots in subjective experiences of perception, thinking, and belief. One can infer the presence of psychosis from manifest behavior, but it is generally through communicative language that hallucinations, delusional convictions, and formal disorders of thought are revealed to the examiner. In general, symptoms in psychotic individuals are more difficult to assess than symptoms in nonpsychotic individuals because, in psychotic conditions, the very cognitive functions that allow communication are often impaired by the disorder. While this is so in adults, it is even more so in children and adolescents in whom language functioning is still developing (Mussen et al.

1979). Psychotic children should be even more difficult to assess than nonpsychotic children and psychotic adults. Given the central relationship of reliability to validity (Spitzer et al. 1978), this is an added complication not generally encountered in adults. The fact that cognitive impairment, including impaired language functioning, is common in psychotic children (Kolvin 1971; Kolvin et al. 1971a–e) makes this factor even more problematic.

Systematic research is needed to develop reliable and valid methods of assessing psychotic phenomena in children. This must start, it seems, with the study of children's use of language.

Cognitive and Social Immaturity of Children: Impact on Symptomatology

When children report symptoms of psychosis, as discussed above, one is faced with the question of assessing the precise psychopathological import of such reported symptoms. Children's cognitive and psychosocial immaturity again adds complications to this process which are encountered less or not at all in the assessment of adults.

Development of Reality Sense. Symptoms that are most prominent in modern diagnostic schemes for schizophrenia are certain types of hallucinations and delusions. These symptoms reveal a patient's defect in the capacity to correctly interpret external reality, despite consensus that holds such beliefs to have no basis in reality: hallucinations involving belief in the verity of *perceptions* in the absence of external stimulus, and delusions involving belief in the truth of *convictions* with no basis in reality. This orientation toward consensual reality has a developmental course through childhood and adolescence. Piaget (see Gruber and Voneche 1977, p 130–138) describes how the process by which "a child replaces his own individual and egocentric point of view by the point of view of others and the reciprocity existing between them" (p 136) continues into adolescence and adulthood. In fact, fantasy play, with its temporary suspension of reality orientation, is characteristic of middle childhood: Bleuler's (1950) description of childhood fantasy play as "normal" autistic thinking reflects this.

In our work with children diagnosed as having prepubertal major depressive disorder (Chambers et al. 1982), we found an unusually high incidence of reported hallucinations: 48 percent reported any hallucination and 36 percent reported complex auditory hallucinations, all experienced in clear consciousness. These experienced hallucinations were much more common in prepubertal children with major depression than in other series of adolescents and adults diagnosed similarly (Table 1). This may indicate a particular susceptibility of children to psychotic-like experiences, particularly hallucinations, because of their immature development of a reality orientation, a cognitive function.

Despert (1940, 1948) addressed this issue in two studies comparing the incidence and characteristics of hallucinatory and delusional phenomena in normal, neurotic, and psychotic children. Her findings were:

1. Normal preschool children show no evidence of true hallucinations or delusions as found in psychotic adults.
2. What were classified as true hallucinations and delusions were found in a small number of neurotic and behavior-disordered children over seven years of age. These symptoms were relatively "segregated" from the rest of the child's mental functions, with the remainder of personality functioning remaining unaffected; were simple of content; and were comprehensible in terms of their content in the context of the child's life situation. In some, one could postulate an adaptive function of the hallucinations and delusions.
3. In "psychotic" children, hallucinations and delusions were found much more frequently, and above 10 years of age they came to resemble similar symptoms in adult psychotics except for their greater simplicity and lack of systematization, similar to phenomena reported by Eggers (1978).

The absence of hallucinations in preschool normal children appears to contradict a hypothesis that immature development of the capacity to test reality predisposes children to psychosis. However, the data are consistent with a hypothesis of interaction of two factors: a) a developmental cognitive immaturity that is largely silent or undetected and b) a superimposed psychiatric disorder, interacting to produce psychosis where neither alone suffices (see Neuchterlein and Dawson, 1984b).

Psychotic Symptoms as Continua Functions. Discrete diagnoses, upon which rational treatment must rest, must be based on

Table 1. Characteristics of Psychotic Symptoms in Children, Adolescents, and Adults

Sample characteristic	Present finding	Source Strober et al. (1981)[a]	Baker et al. (1971)
N	58	40	100
N with psychotic symptoms	29 (48%)	5 (12.5%)	
Age range, years	6–12	12–17	16–76
Mean age, years	9.31	15.04	45.9
Auditory hallucinations			
N	28 (48%)	4 (10%)	9 (9%)
Affective	20 (34%)	4 (10%)	—
Nonaffective	1 (2%)	0 (0%)	—
Themes			
Command	18 (31%)	0 (0%)	—
Conversing	2 (3%)	0 (0%)	—
Persecution	8 (14%)	4 (10%)	—
Religious	3 (5%)	0 (0%)	—
Other verbal	5 (9%)	0 (0%)	—
Delusions			
N	4 (7%)	5 (12.5%)	27 (27%)
Depressive	3 (5%)	5 (12.5%)	16 (16%)
Nondepressive	2 (3%)	0 (0%)	14 (14%)
Themes			
Sin, guilt	2 (3%)	5 (12.5%)	—
Punishment, persecution	1 (2%)	5 (12.5%)	—
Nihilism	2 (3%)	2 (5%)	—
Somatic	0 (0%)	2 (5%)	—
Control	1 (2%)	0 (0%)	—
Grandiosity	1 (2%)	0 (0%)	—

[a] Published data from Strober et al. (1981); further data provided by Strober (written communication, January 14, 1982).

Reprinted with permission from Chambers WJ, Puig-Antich J, Tabrizi MA, et al: Psychotic symptoms in prepubertal major depressive disorder. Archives of General Psychiatry 39:921-927. Copyright 1982, American Medical Association.

the presence or absence of particular symptoms. In physical medicine, signs generally exist along continua, with defined cutoff points distinguishing pathology from normality. In psychiatry, diagnostic schemes are based on discrete entities: symptoms such as hallucinations, delusions, and formal thinking disorder for schizophrenia. Are they indeed discrete phenomena, defined along a strict present–absent dimension, or do they exist along continua defined by dimensions of severity or intensity? While diagnostic schemes treat psychiatric symptoms as discrete entities, there is some evidence they do exist along continua of severity. There is, furthermore, reason to believe that viewing symptoms of psychoses in children and adolescents as points on continua is more important than it may be in adults, because of the unique cognitive characteristics of children. Several diagnostic instruments for adults, in their assessment schemes for psychotic disorders, adopt a viewpoint of a continuum.

1. "Pseudohallucinations" have been historically distinguished from "true" hallucinations according to two criteria: location experienced as emanating from within or outside the head (Jaspers 1963a, 1963b; Koehler 1979; Schneider 1959; Wing et al. 1974) and the degree of insight the subject possessed into the reality of the experience (E. Bleuler in Koehler 1979).
2. Other phenomena include "partial" delusions and "questionable" delusions and hallucinations. In the Present State Examination (PSE; Wing et al. 1974), in addition to true hallucinations and delusions, one is able to rate the presence of questionable hallucinations and delusions (phenomena inquired about but whose presence cannot be definitely ascertained) and partial delusions (delusional ideas are expressed with doubt instead of with conviction). In the schizophrenia patient cohort of the International Pilot Study of Schizophrenia, which used the PSE, Strauss (1969) found half as many questionable delusions as true delusions and three quarters as many questionable hallucinations as full hallucinations. Strauss interprets these results as indicating that psychotic

symptoms in adult schizophrenics exist along continua and not as discrete phenomena.

3. Chapman and Chapman (1980) developed an 11-point scale rating psychotic-like experiences in adults from normal to psychotic. They claim that this is a scale for rating experiences and not a diagnostic instrument; it is, in essence, a scale for classifying psychotic-like symptomatology.

4. Endicott and Spitzer (1978) have developed the Schedule for Affective Disorders and Schizophrenia (SADS) for the National Institute of Mental Health Collaborative Study on the Psychobiology of Depression. In SADS, both hallucinations and delusions are rated along a six-point continuum of severity defined by degree of conviction in the abnormal experience and the impact that the experience has on the patient's life.

5. Koehler (1979) has proposed that Schneiderian first-rank symptoms be rated along three continua (three to seven points each) that he has devised.

The question of whether psychotic symptoms in adults are best conceived of as discrete entities or as points on continua is unanswered, and is considerably more complex in children. How does one define as pathological a symptom or phenomenon characterized, in part, by a defect in capacity that normally may not yet be fully developed at the age in question? The problem of defining the boundaries between normal and pathological phenomena is considerable.

Phenomena involving a suspension of orientation toward consensual reality are normally found in children's fantasy play. Bleuler (1950) describes this as normal "autistic" thinking (p 374). Childhood phenomena such as imaginary companions (Bender and Vogel 1941); pseudohallucinations (Egdell and Kolvin 1972); elaborated fantasy (Despert 1940, 1948); images (Egdell and Kolvin 1972); and eidetic imagery (Egdell and Kolvin 1972) all share some features with hallucinations and delusions.

In our previously cited study of prepubertal children diagnosed as major depressive disorder (Chambers et al. 1982), the 48 percent of the sample reporting auditory hallucinations believed in the veracity of those experiences with a wide range of conviction. Eleven of 28 children (39 percent) believed the hallucination was "generally his imagination and able to ignore it." The remaining 17 held the belief with greater conviction, ranging from mild to absolute.

Other parameters that may be rated along continua are frequency, location from which hallucinations appear to be emanating, bizarreness of content, severity of presumed precipitating stress, and degree to which the psychotic process or symptoms interfere with general personality functioning. (This latter parameter could be rated along a bidirectional scale reflecting whether the hallucinations fostered or disrupted normal personality functioning, that is, promoted adaptation.) It is largely untested whether such parameters have psychopathological importance. One piece of data derives from the study of prepubertal major depressive disorder cited previously: Children with any psychotic form of the disorder (primarily hallucinating children) required higher plasma levels of imipramine plus desipramine to achieve therapeutic resolution of the depressive syndrome (Puig-Antich et al. in press). The precise psychopathological import of less-than-severe points on graded continua (the two types of pseudohallucinations, for example) as to their relation to outcome and treatment response are as yet unclear.

Susceptibility to Being Influenced: Social Dependency and Immaturity. Several authors have reported that psychotic symptoms (primarily hallucinations) in children are etiologically related to external influences: When the children are removed from the noxious setting or influence, the symptoms resolve. Influences described include stress in general (Eisenberg 1962); poverty and its attendant stresses (Bender and Lipkowitz 1940; Edgell and Kolvin 1972); and subculturally held religious beliefs, particularly religious beliefs and practices (Wilking and Paoli 1966). Poverty is particularly important, considering the generally low social class found in cohorts of adult (Hollingshead and Redlich 1958) and childhood (Kolvin et al. 1971b) schizophrenics. Subcultural beliefs, including the beliefs in spiritualism and seances, are becoming increasingly prominent in the United States, with recently increasing migration from Caribbean and Central American nations with prominent spiritualist traditions and practices (Canino and Bird 1981). Clearly, if hallucinations (and delusions) are among the most important symptoms for diagnosing schizophrenia, and if their appearance can be influenced by sociocultural events or forces, then these events or forces must be taken into account in assessing children for a schizophrenia diagnosis.

These reports of hallucinatory episodes occurring in response to specific stressors have resulted in the rather odd concept of hallucinations occurring in nonpsychotic children and adolescents. Because the two states (being hallucinating and nonpsychotic) appear to be mutually exclusive, some explanation must be available. Reading of the case reports of such children reveals that a) the hallucinations occurred as isolated phenomena in children whose capacity to relate to others was unimpaired and b) the themes of the hallucinations were generally grounded in the reality of the child's life situation (or wished-for life situation). Similarly, those cases reported by Despert (1948) were seen as aiding psychological adaptation. This is in marked contrast to hallucinations in schizophrenic individuals in whom the hallucinations are maladaptive, bear little relationship to one's reality orientation, and are part of a generalized disruption of psychological processes, which include the capacity for human relatedness. The hallucinations described in nonpsychotic children are thus described as fundamentally different from those occurring in psychotic people.

A fundamental issue is unclear: whether this difference is qualitative or quantitative. Do the hallucinations in nonpsychotic children under stress reflect a process fundamentally different from that for hallucinations occurring in psychotics, or are they merely the mild end of a continuum of severity of psychotic illnesses? In adults, the previously made distinction between "good prognosis" and "process" schizophrenia is becoming blurred as follow-up studies proceed (Vaillant 1978). The reports of nonpsychotic hallucinating children indicate that they do recover fully from their hallucinations when the stress is removed. However, these children are only at the earliest point in the age of risk for schizophrenia, and follow-up on them has been brief. Systematic, long-term follow-up studies of such nonpsychotic children well into the age of risk have not been done and are necessary before one can conclude that such nonpsychotic hallucinating children have disorders qualitatively and fundamentally different from process psychotic disorders.

A third possibility is that nonpsychotic hallucinating children are immaturely developed in the cognitive capacity for reality testing, which may be at the root of schizophrenic pathology, and that their generally good prognosis reflects that this capacity ultimately develops. Most of these children do not grow up to be schizophrenic or chronically psychotic. The other side of the coin is that the children who hallucinate in stressful circumstances represent a minority of children who experience the stresses described. Such children might thus profitably be the subjects of detailed study, including cross-sectional neuropsychological and follow-up assessments, using a multi-axial diagnostic scheme.

The *DSM-III* criteria for the diagnosis of schizophrenia or schizophreniform psychosis in children and adolescents probably are too broad. To be diagnosed as schizophrenic disorder by *DSM-III*, a child or adolescent could have a behavior disorder (nonhallucinating) in response to a serious life stressor, with impaired school performance, for six months and experience ego-syntonic nonaffective hallucinations (without personality disruption) several times a day for a week or two. Several of the children described as nonpsychotic in the previously cited reports could thus, by *DSM-III*, be diagnosed (inappropriately, I think) as schizophrenic. The most important distinction to be made in this regard would appear to be the extent to which the hallucinations were part of a general process of personality disorganization. This is, however, only a clinical hunch and should be the subject of research.

The diagnostic imprecision referred to above thus results, it seems, from the adverse impact of children's immature cognitive and psychosocial development on either the symptomatic manifestations of their illness or on the diagnostic process itself. The central research issue appears to be primarily one of measurement:

assessing parameters in the cognitive and psychosocial spheres, which may be a) difficult to define clearly and systematically and thus very difficult to measure reliably and b) developing at variable rates and at different times in children in the age range being studied.

These issues are only just now becoming the subject of systematic research. Areas that appear to this author to be most critical in this regard are a) measurement of the ability to test reality; b) identification of cognitive capacities that are related functionally to the capacity for testing reality, whether in psychotic or normal individuals, children or adults; c) development of instruments for the reliable assessment of psychotic phenomena in children; and d) validation of the self-reports of children and adolescents on their psychotic symptomatology and measurement of the degree of development of a consensual versus an egocentric orientation in interpersonal communications. Modern research has only begun to address these issues.

Piaget studied the development of an orientation toward consensual versus egocentric reality (Inhelder and Piaget 1958). The methods used in these studies are, however, difficult to operationalize in a way so as to be useful in the study of psychotic children. Recently, Foley et al. (1983) and Johnson and Raye (1981) studied aspects of this process in normal children and adolescents. They define "reality monitoring" as "the process of discriminating between self-generated memories and memories produced by perceptual processing of external events" (Foley et al. 1983, p 51). They tested the Piagetian notion that the ability to distinguish imagined from actually perceived memories develops with age. They found no evidence for any difference between children 6 to 8 years old and late adolescents or adults in this capacity as it related to visual imaginings versus perceived pictures, and to their own words versus those they had heard.

Another series of experiments, however, revealed one capacity that does show developmental differences between 6 and 17 years of age—the capacity to distinguish what they actually said from what they themselves only thought—whereas there were no differences in ability to distinguish what they only thought from what someone else said to them. Foley et al. (1983, p 58) thus concluded that "cues for differentiating the self from others in memory may be well developed in quite young children" (6 years of age). However, the capacity for distinguishing memories of what one said from what one only thought ("self-generated memories differing in their degree of realization," p 58) is a much more complex task and is less well developed in 6-year-olds. The source of this latter difference is unclear. Furthermore, these capacities have not been compared between hallucinating psychotic and hallucinating nonpsychotic children, those with nonhallucinatory psychiatric disorders and normals. Thus, the relevance of the capacities being studied to the questions regarding reality testing in psychoses remains uncertain.

Asarnow and Sherman (1984) have conducted ongoing studies of the capacities for information processing in schizophrenic adults and children in comparison with normals. This reflects one of the few attempts to systematically study defects of reality testing in children, adolescents, and adults fulfilling *DSM-III* criteria for schizophrenia, attempting to control for developmental factors. Asarnow and Sherman have identified a deficit of attentional capacities that appears in schizophrenic children. This is consistent with a body of data on cognitive deficits in schizophrenic adults and children at risk for schizophrenia (Chapman 1979; Neuchterlein and Dawson 1984a; Rutschmann et al. 1977). The work of Foley and Johnson is important in that it is directly relevant to the cognitive processes that relate to productive secondary symptoms of schizophrenic and other psychotic disorders: the capacity to correctly interpret reality.

CHILDHOOD SCHIZOPHRENIA

The diagnosis of psychotic disorders in children has a long history, dating from the description by Sancte de Sanctis (1906/1969) of children affected with "dementia praecoxissima," a disorder he related to Bleuler's "dementia praecox" (1950) in adults. The study of childhood psychosis since de Sanctis's time has been reviewed by Werry (1979) and will be only briefly reviewed here. Suffice it to say that the issue of definition of *childhood schizophrenia* was chaotic until 1943. By his separation of the syndrome of infantile autism from the group of disorders previously lumped together as childhood schizophrenia, Kanner made a fundamental distinction that persists to this day. Primarily as a result of Kolvin's (1971) study, autism was removed from the schizophrenic disorders classification and is now classified in *DSM–III* as a disorder of neurocognitive development. Even the venerable *Journal of Autism and Childhood Schizophrenia* has been renamed the *Journal of Autism and Developmental Disorders.*

After Kolvin's (1971) study, the childhood psychoses were classified into three groups: the infantile psychoses related to autism; the rare degenerative psychoses related to degenerative brain diseases; and the late-onset psychoses (LOP), thought to represent early-onset schizophrenia, with onset of psychosis (however *psychosis* is defined) after five years of age (Rutter 1974). This distinction has been generally accepted and is incorporated into *DSM–III*, though the distinction of autism as a disorder distinct from schizophrenia has not been universally accepted. Some follow-up studies (Howells and Giurguis 1984; Petty et al. 1984) of autistic children reveal diagnoses of schizophrenia in adulthood. Whereas these cases may represent a subgroup of autistics who grow up to be schizophrenic, some become similar to simple schizophrenics with a clinical picture similar to grown-up autistics (Eisenberg 1957). Those grown-up autistics who have typical productive schizophrenic symptoms (hallucinations, delusions, formal thinking disorder) are a very small minority of grown-up autistics. Furthermore, they have not been shown to occur more often than the 1 percent prevalence expected in the general population. Nobody has suggested that autism confers immunity to other diseases, including schizophrenia. Family pedigree studies of autistics are in process but at this time are inconclusive.

The late-onset psychoses are generally agreed to represent early-onset forms of adult-type schizophrenia, even among those who believe that autism may represent early-onset schizophrenia. It is this presumption of the equivalence of LOP with schizophrenia that will be reviewed. Only nine studies (of which I am aware) in the English language literature since 1943 support this conclusion. These are the studies of Annell (1963); Bender (1942, 1953, 1959, 1970, 1971, 1974, 1975) and Bender et al. (1952, 1956); Cantor et al. (1979, 1980, 1981); Eggers (1978); Green et al. (1984); Kallman and Roth (1956); Kolvin (1971) and Kolvin et al. (1971a, 1971b, 1971c, 1971d, 1971e); Makita (1966); and Vrono (1973/1974).

Because hallucinations have been fundamental to the diagnosis of LOP and schizophrenia in most modern diagnostic schemes, a review of the concept of late-onset psychoses of childhood and adolescence is indicated.

Diagnostic Criteria

The presumption incorporated into *DSM-III* is that criteria for schizophrenia in adults apply to children as well. The situation regarding diagnostic criteria for schizophrenia in children is complicated by two factors:

1. There is no agreement at this time as to the most valid criteria for schizophrenia in adults. Criteria have been proposed by a number of groups (American Psychiatric Association 1980; Astrachan et al. 1972; Carpenter et al. 1973; Schneider 1959; Spitzer et al. 1978; Wing et al. 1974).

2. Whereas the issue of diagnostic criteria for schizophrenia in adults remains unsettled, the issue with regard to children has never been studied. The nine cited studies of LOP used diagnostic criteria that were widely divergent from each other (Table 2). They range from Annell (1963), an extremely experienced prominent Swedish child psychiatrist who made a diagnosis of "psychotic syndrome" relying upon a "subjective estimate of the symptoms shown by the child" (p 237), to Kolvin et al. (1971a), who relied on a strict Schneiderian system, and Cantor (1979, 1980, 1981) and Green et al. (1984), who used *DSM-III* criteria.

In sum, some authors have concluded that "it is evident that all psychiatrists do not have the same state of illness in mind when they speak of Schizophrenie" (Annell 1963, p 236), whereas others

Table 2. Diagnostic Criteria: Studies of Late-Onset Psychoses

Study	Criteria
Annell (1963)	It has . . . proved impossible to find a definition satisfying everybody [for "psychotic syndrome"]. No precise symptom or combination of symptoms exists which classifies a state of sickness as psychotic. The selection of the primary material was consequently made by a subjective estimate of the symptoms. . . . The term psychosis or psychotic syndrome has been used in the broad sense; where a doubt existed whether a psychosis was present, the case was included in the material (p 237–238).
Bender (1947)	Our own definition of childhood schizophrenia has been a clinical entity, occurring in childhood before the age of eleven years, which reveals pathology in behavior at every level and in every area of integration or patterning within the functioning of the central nervous system, be it vegetable, motor, perceptual, intellectual, emotional, or social. Furthermore, this behavior pathology disturbs the pattern of every functioning field in a characteristic way. The pathology cannot therefore be thought of as focal in the architecture of the central nervous system, but rather as striking at the substratum of integrative functioning or biologically patterned behavior. (p 40)
Eggers (1978)	The term childhood schizophrenia has to be clarified. Unlike some authors we do not include psychotic-like temper tantrums of brain injured children and/or oligophrenic children, early infantile autism, severe psychoneurotic disorders or neurotically determined delay or deviation of ego development. . . . We diagnose a psychotic disorder in a child as "schizophrenic" only if clear schizophrenic symptoms, as found in adult schizophrenia, are present. (p 21–22)
Kallman and Roth (1956)	The diagnostic criteria for index cases . . . were generally on the conservative side. . . . A distinct change in the behavior of a child who previously seemed to develop normally was regarded as a crucial diagnostic feature. (p 600)
Kolvin et al. (1971a)	Our ascertainment criteria were: 1. Onset during the main school period of five to fifteen. 2. Adult schizophrenic symptoms of the first rank (Schneider). [Symptoms are listed.] 3. Other adult schizophrenic symptoms in the fields of affect, motility and volition. (p 384)
Makita (1966)	Fifty cases of schizophrenic disorder under the age of fifteen diagnosed as such in the Children's Psychiatric Service at Keio University Hospital . . . comprise the case materials. (p 112) [Cases of infantile autism and Mahler's symbiotic psychosis are included.]
Vrono (1973/1974)	Soviet psychiatrists have viewed childhood schizophrenia as a single nosological entity, defined by the same criteria as other mental illnesses: namely, common etiology, pathogenesis, clinical picture, course, and outcome. (p 10)
Cantor et al. (1979, 1980, 1981)	*Diagnostic and Statistical Manual of Mental Disorders (Third Edition)* (DSM-III; American Psychiatric Association 1980)
Green et al. (1984)	*DSM-III*

have used a more systemized criteria set, be it Schneiderian (Kolvin et al. 1971a) or *DSM-III* (Cantor 1979, 1981; Green et al. 1984).

Bender's (1947) criteria occupy an intermediate position between Annell's subjective estimate and the more systematic criteria, that is, the *DSM-III* and Schneiderian. Bender's criteria have been criticized (Eisenberg 1957) as too vague and incapable of being applied generally; and Makita (1966) presented no criteria. Most of these studies were performed at a time when the precise specification of diagnostic criteria was not common practice, and the criteria were generally made according to the prevailing clinical thought in a country. However, when viewed against modern standards (*DSM-III*, for example), the studies are difficult to compare with each other. It is unclear, for instance, how much overlap there would be among groups of children diagnosed as schizophrenic by the nine investigators of most of the cited studies, because of the nature of the reports of diagnostic criteria. Hallucinations are included in the diagnostic criteria of four of the nine studies, those of Eggers (1978), Kolvin et al. (1971a–e), Cantor et al. (1979, 1980, 1981) and Green et al. (1984). The remaining studies of Annell, Bender, Kallman and Roth, and Makita do not appear to have relied on precisely defined symptom criteria.

The *DSM-III* task force made a presumption: that adult criteria, largely Schneiderian in origin, apply equally to children. The above discussion raises serious questions about this in that the assessment of psychotic phenomena in children is complicated by two factors: the relatively (relative to normal adults) undeveloped capacity of reality testing in children and the difficulties inflicted on the measurement of psychotic phenomena by children's immature cognitive and psychosocial development. The issue can be tested by looking to the nine studies of late-onset psychoses and asking the question, Do the data of those nine studies, particularly the studies using specified modern (Schneiderian) criteria, support or refute the equivalence of late-onset psychoses with schizophrenia? This is an issue akin to the research for validating parameters for a diagnosis of schizophrenia in adults.

To this date, only the platelet monoamine oxidase (MAO) level offers the greatest potential as a biological marker (validator) for the diagnosis of schizophrenia. However, this has not been proven to identify all or a subgroup of schizophrenics, and no study has yet measured platelet MAO in well-defined LOP children. We are thus left with three independent validators of the diagnosis of schizophrenia in LOP children: follow-up rediagnosis after adolescence (the first period of increased risk), psychosocial functioning or adaptation on follow-up, and family incidence of mental illness.

Psychotic Forms of Affective Disorder

Before attempting by these parameters to independently validate or refute the conclusion of the equivalence of LOP with schizophrenia, a question regarding diagnostic criteria must be addressed: In the nine studies, including those with Schneiderian criteria, were psychotic forms of other psychiatric disorders ruled out? It is possible that because of children's possibly increased likelihood to report hallucinations, psychotic forms of other *DSM-III* Axis One disorders must be ruled out. The *DSM-III* specifically notes affective disorders as an exclusion criterion for the diagnosis of schizophrenia. Seven of the nine LOP studies were performed before a consensus was reached that adult-type affective disorders occur in prepuberty and adolescence (Puig-Antich et al. 1983), including psychiatric forms of affective disorder (Chambers et al. 1982; Freeman et al. 1985; Burke et al. 1985).

The studies of Cantor et al. (1979, 1980, 1981) and Green et al. (1984) were published after childhood-onset affective disorders were recognized. The LOP subjects of Green et al. (1984) were collected between 1977 and 1982 and were diagnosed by retrospective chart review and behavioral observations. Absence of affective disorder is not specifically described in this report. The consensus is emerging (Chambers et al. 1985; Puig-Antich and Gittelman 1982) that a direct, semistructured or structured interview with a child for affective disorder symptoms is essential to the diagnosis of affective disorder in children. All these considerations leave open the possibility that affective disorder may have been overlooked in this sample. Cantor et al. (1979, 1980, 1981) used a symptom checklist for diagnosis. None of the symptoms of the depressive syndrome (American Psychiatric Association 1980; Spitzer et al. 1978) were questioned or assessed with this checklist. Although fulfillment of *DSM-III* criteria for schizophrenia (which includes exclusion of affective disorder) is described, the lack of described systematic assessment by direct interview for affective disorder leaves the question of the possible presence of affectively disordered patients in this sample unclear. The studies of Cantor and Green are thus inconclusive as to the possibility of childhood psychotic affective disorders being present within their samples. Both samples were collected before descriptions of psychotic forms of childhood affective disorder were first published (Chambers et al. 1982), however.

The question then arises in the seven remaining studies of LOP whether there is evidence for the unrecognized presence of affective disorder because the occurrence of major affective disorder in children and adolescents was not recognized at the time the studies were performed.

Three of the nine studies present data in a way that is useful in this regard. Kolvin et al.'s (1971b) data weakly support this hypothesis. They report that "a small number of the LOP cases tended to become easily depressed" (p 392) and 19 percent of the parents of LOP children showed what was, admittedly loosely defined, "depressive neurotic disorder," though 16 percent of parents of infantile psychotic (autistic) children did also. The pattern of occurrence of symptoms of psychosis in Kolvin's sample were hallucinations (81 percent); formal thinking disorder (60 percent with disorders of association, 45 percent with derailment, 24 percent with autistic thinking, 51 percent with talking past the point, and 60 percent showing thought blocking); and delusions (57 percent). This is not dissimilar to the pattern in adult schizophrenic patients in the International Pilot Study of Schizophrenia (IPSS; World Health Organization 1973), though Kolvin's series reported a higher incidence of auditory hallucinations (81 percent versus 42 percent) than the adult sample. Persecutory delusions were reported in 51.8 percent of the IPSS adult sample and 42 percent of Kolvin's sample of children. This may reflect an increased likelihood for children to report hallucinations but not delusions.

Eggers and Vrono presented more detailed clinical data. Eggers (1978) reported that in 55 percent of his 57 cases, prodromal features preceded the psychosis, and "states of depressive mood were most common" (p 30). During the prodromal phase, three combinations of symptoms proved statistically significant: depressive/weeping without a reason, delusions/excitement, and delusions/weeping with a reason. There was "a considerable risk of suicide" (p 30) in the prodromal phase: Seven children expressed suicidal ideas or made attempts. Eggers further observes: "The occurrence of cyclothymic [depressive, manic, manic-depressive] phases and prodromal episodes characterized 26 [of 57] patients [46%]; these appeared before the onset of the schizophrenic psychosis or alternated with schizophrenic episodes" (p 30). Furthermore, "three cases of *schizophrenia* later appeared as cases of *depressive psychosis* 3, 7, and 8 years after the appearance of the schizophrenic psychosis" (italics added). Eggers further notes that 65 percent of the patients were preoccupied with death: During the psychosis 14 (25 percent) expressed death thoughts, 15 percent had suicidal intentions without acts, 20 percent attempted suicide, and 5 percent committed suicide. Thus, Eggers's data, though suggestive that patients with affective disorder may have been included in this LOP sample, are no more than suggestive, for affective symptoms are commonly described in cohorts of schizophrenic subjects.

Vrono (1973/1974) is the only author of the seven cited studies of LOP who presents clinical cases in detail. His case histories cover several years of illness for 10 patients, illustrating various forms of what he classifies as a unitary disorder childhood schizophrenia. The author extracted symptoms relevant to the *DSM-III* diagnoses of schizophrenia, depression, and mania, and then plotted the reported symptoms for one or two periods of described illness in each case reported (Table 3). It must be remembered that only symptoms reported as present or absent or judged likely to be

Table 3. *DSM-III* Symptoms of Schizophrenia Extracted From Reported Symptoms in Vrono's (1973/1974) Cases of Late-Onset Psychoses

Symptom	Case										
	1 Females 6–16 years	2 Males 3–15 years	3 Females 6–11 years	4 Females 5–19 years	5 Males 12–15 years	6 Males 13 years	7 Males 13 years	7 Males 15 years	8 Males 13–15 years	9 Females 15 years	10 Females 15–17 years
Hallucination				P						P	P
Delusion			P			P			P	P	P
Formal thought disorder									P		L
Bizarre behavior									P		
Dysphoria (+4)	P	P	P	P		P				P	P
Anhedonia	L	P				P		P			
Insomnia				P	P						P
Fatigue	P					O					
Psychomotor	P	P	P	P	P	P			P	P	
Anorexia				P	P	P					
Guilt						L			P	P	
Concentration	P			O		O					P
Suicide				P		P	P				P
Elation (+4)							P		P		P
Irritability (+5)			P			P	P		P		
Hyperactivity			P			P	L				
Talkativeness			P								
Flight of ideas			P						P		
Grandiosity							P		P		
Decreased need of sleep							L		P		
Distractible	P						P				
Poor judgment		P					P				

Note. P = present at least once; L = likely present; O = reported absent. If space is blank, presence or absence was not reported.

present are recorded here. A blank space means either that the symptom was absent or that it was present but not recorded by Vrono.

Review of the cases reveals that 4 of the 10 patients had no *DSM-III* "characteristic" symptoms of schizophrenia reported: no hallucinations, delusions, formal thinking disorders, or bizarre behavior (Cases 1, 2, 5, and 7). Of these 4, Case 1 likely fulfills criteria for depressive disorder, Case 7 likely fulfills criteria for manic disorder, and Case 2 has depressed mood and two of the required four symptoms of the depressive syndrome. The remaining 6 patients reported hallucinations and/or delusions. Of the 6, Cases 4, 6, and 10 fulfill criteria for depressive disorder by *DSM-III*. Vrono himself diagnosed Case 10 as "schizoaffective disorder," which would be its Research Diagnostic Criteria (RDC; Spitzer et al. 1978) diagnosis as well. Case 9 had depressed mood and two symptoms of the depressive syndrome reported; Case 8 had suggestions of a manic disorder (elation, irritability and two of four required symptoms of the manic syndrome); Case 3 had three of the four requisite symptoms of the manic syndrome, plus elation and irritability reported.

There is thus, in Vrono's data, strong evidence that at least some of the subjects diagnosed as childhood schizophrenic before 1973 might today be diagnosed as suffering from an affective disorder. Carlson and Strober (1978) provide support for this hypothesis: Six children diagnosed as schizophrenic between 12 and 16 years of age were, on follow-up, diagnosed with RDC as suffering from mania or depression. The possibility exists that in the era before major affective disorder was found to occur in children and adolescents, a number of the cases reported by Chambers et al. (1982), Strober et al. (1981), and Freeman et al. (1985) may have been diagnosed as schizophrenic.

The discovery of what proportion of hallucinating or psychotic children may have a concurrent treatable affective disorder must await future research. In our psychopharmacology study of prepubertal depression (Puig-Antich et al. in press), the symptoms of psychosis always resolved when the episode of affective disorder resolved.

VALIDATING PARAMETERS

With an independent variable so unreliable and elusive as that of schizophrenia occurring in children, one must turn to parameters independent of childhood diagnosis to attempt to validate that diagnosis. Three parameters are currently available for this purpose: rediagnosis after follow-up through adolescence (to presumably eliminate the effects of cognitive and psychosocial immaturity in childhood), social functioning on follow-up, and family incidence of mental illness.

Rediagnosis After Adolescence

Subsequent course has long been a validating criterion for a diagnosis of schizophrenia in adults. However, this generally refers to the frequency of relapse and the degree of recovery or restitution attained. In considering a diagnosis of schizophrenia made in childhood, however, one is subject to all the pitfalls of assessment and diagnosis in children discussed previously. It is thus essential in validating the childhood diagnosis to follow the course of the illness through the adolescent years when a more typical adult pattern of illness would become established (Eggers 1978) and the assessment pitfalls of childhood would be passed.

Eggers (1978) and Bender (1970) studied course in their samples. Eggers followed up 71 children who had been diagnosed as schizophrenic between ages 7 and 13 years for an average of 15 years, all but 7 by direct interview. Twenty-five of 71 cases, a full 35 percent, either had complete or almost complete recovery or a nonpsychotic diagnosis on follow-up. Eleven of the 25 (15 percent of the sample) were completely normal after being diagnosed schizophrenic in childhood. Forty-six of the 71 cases (65 percent) had a psychotic diagnosis on follow-up, ranging from recurrent psychoses with full interepisode recovery to a severe schizophrenic defect state.

Eggers eliminated 14 cases from the analysis because of doubt on follow-up as to the verity of the original diagnosis, or the appearance of temporal lobe epilepsy or neurologic signs, and so forth, in the remaining 54 cases (Eggers 1978; Eggers C: personal communication, July 3, 1979). Eggers classified the course of the psychotic disorders into acute–relapsing and chronic courses in follow-ups averaging 15 years. Sixty-four percent of cases with onset at or before 10 years of age followed a chronic course. Cases that subsequently followed a chronic course much less frequently showed hallucinations (and delusions) than cases following an acute– relapsing course (later onset). However, both showed productive psychotic symptoms on follow-up. Thus, hallucinations in adolescent-onset psychosis in Eggers's sample predict an acute–relapsing course. It is conceivable that these acute–relapsing cases could represent unrecognized cases of psychotic affective disorders similar to Strober et al.'s (1981) cases.

Bender's (1970) data show that 87 percent of the children whom she located after 16 years were rediagnosed schizophrenic. However, 44 percent were diagnosed by the staff of another institution, generally a state hospital, without being seen by the research staff. This is a poor standard on which to base the validity of research findings. Because of this it seems wise to consider these findings interesting but in need of verification. Eggers personally interviewed all but seven (10 percent) of his sample, and his results are thus that much more interesting.

Social Functioning on Follow-Up

Four studies, those of Annell (1963), Bender (1970), Eggers (1978), and Vrono (1973/1974), followed social outcome after adolescence. The first issue to be addressed concerns which measures of outcome were used. Recent years have seen the development of rigorous methods for evaluating social outcome in adult schizophrenics, most notably those developed by Strauss and Carpenter (1972) and the IPSS (World Health Organization 1973, 1979). Because follow-up of the child samples extends into young adulthood, the same outcome parameters are applicable as in adult studies. The specific parameters used in the four childhood studies vary widely among themselves, and none bears a close similarity to the adult parameters of Strauss and Carpenter or the IPSS.

The results of the four studies are nonetheless provocative. In all of the four studies, despite widely varying criteria of diagnosis and outcome, the social outcomes vary over a wide range.

Annell (1963) studied work and living situation at follow-up in 62 subjects diagnosed as schizophrenic in childhood and adolescence. She found that 16 (26 percent) were working, 13 (21 percent) were working but with behavior problems, 2 (3 percent) were delinquent but not incarcerated at that time, 6 (10 percent) were cared for by their families, and 25 (40 percent) were institutionalized.

Bender (1970) studied 100 children and adolescents diagnosed as having childhood schizophrenia, at an interval of 16–33 years, when they were 22 to 46 years of age. Of the 100 patients, 35 were continuously hospitalized, and 28 had a history of intermittent hospitalization. Of these 63, 27 were diagnosed as autistic (and schizophrenic), and 36 had illnesses with pubertal onset. The remaining 37 were living in the community and showed variable levels of adjustment.

Eggers (1978) made global ratings of social functioning in the 57 cases diagnosed as childhood schizophrenia on follow-up of 15 years. It is to be recalled that 14 additional cases were excluded from analysis at follow-up because of doubts as to the original diagnosis of childhood schizophrenia; their follow-up disorders were essentially neurotic or neurological. Of the 57 cases, Eggers found that 11 (19 percent) showed complete remission and full recovery, 18 (32 percent) showed "good to very good" functioning, 10 (18 percent) showed "fair to poor" functioning, 12 (21 percent) functioned at a "very poor" level, and 6 (10 percent) showed a schizophrenic defect state. Eggers found that cases with onset of psychosis under 10 years of age had a uniformly poor prognosis.

Vrono (1973/1974) reported on the capacity for work at follow-up of 5 to over 20 years on 200 patients who had been diagnosed as schizophrenic in childhood and adolescence. Thirty-one (15.5 percent) were fully able to work, 56 (28 percent) had reduced work capacity, 41 (20.5 percent) had partially lost their work capacity, and 72 (36 percent) had completely lost their work capacity and required continuous care and supervision. There was a tendency for those with onset of schizophrenia before 13 years of age to have a somewhat greater incidence of diminished capacity for work. Thirteen percent with onset before age 13 had intact capacity for work compared with 18 percent for those whose onset was after age 13. Forty percent of those with onset before age 13 required continuous care; 32 percent of those whose onset was after age 13 required continuous care.

A substantial proportion of each sample has very high functioning or full recovery, and a substantial proportion requires continuous care or has developed a malignant defect state. A wide range of social outcome characterizes cohorts of schizophrenic adults as well (World Health Organization 1973, 1979). However, schizophrenia with onset in childhood and adolescence may be thought to represent a more severe or malignant form of illness. There is some support for this hypothesis in the data of Eggers (1978), but the methodological differences between, and limitations of, the studies makes this difficult to interpret. Thus, Eggers found that onset of psychoses before 10 years of age resulted in uniformly poor prognosis, whereas Vrono (1973/1974) found little difference in outcome in children with onset under or over 13 years of age.

The only conclusion is that there may be some evidence that children with onset of schizophrenia-like disorders from 6 through 9 years of age may have particularly malignant forms of the illness, based on Eggers's data. This finding is clearly in need of replication, using modern diagnostic schemes and assessment techniques. Children with onset at so young an age, nonetheless, constitute a small proportion of children with schizophrenia-like psychosis (Kolvin et al. 1971a–e; Makita 1966; Rutter 1974). The authors of the four studies seem to agree that children with onset after age 10, as they approach puberty, who form the majority of children with LOP, have disorders, most of which seem to have a good prognosis. The influence of the developmental process in these years on childhood psychotic disorders is clearly worthy of study.

Review of course of illness in the four cited studies of LOP highlights a central unresolved issue in our existing knowledge of the LOP. Predictive validity is the most important available parameter in validating any diagnostic statement concerning the LOP. By this parameter, the LOP is a heterogeneous disorder particularly for therapeutic and research reasons. There is either one homogeneous condition, the late-onset psychotic disorders, related to schizophrenia, in which prognosis is a result of a number of variables external to diagnosis (neurological dysfunction, intelligence and social class effects, for example); or the LOP are a group of distinct disorders, with distinct patterns of course and outcome, each of which shares certain features (psychotic symptomatology); or the variable outcome is the result of a combination of these two polar concepts. At this point, issues of diagnostic assessment become critical. As the diagnostic nomenclature in child psychiatry becomes increasingly sophisticated and complex, and with the development of specific treatments for specific disorders, the question of the nature of the heterogeneity of the LOP becomes increasingly important, particularly in view of a possible greater susceptibility of prepubertal children to report hallucinations.

Family Incidence of Mental Illness

Family incidence of mental illness has been shown (Tsaung 1979) to be able to distinguish a sample of adult schizophrenics from a group of patients with affective disorders. The utility of family history of mental illness as a validating parameter for a diagnosis of schizophrenia is hampered by the relatively low, though increased, incidence of schizophrenia in relatives of adults with schizophrenia.

Four of the nine cited studies of childhood psychoses reported family mental illness data: the studies of Annell (1963). Annell's data are presented in such a way that the numbers cannot be interpreted. Furthermore, the global terms *psychosis* and *severe mental disturbance* in parents, aunts, uncles, and grandparents are reported: Endogenous depressions, acute alcoholic psychosis, and schizophrenia are included in these heterogeneous groups.

Eggers, in the English summary (1978) of his German-language monograph (1973), reports that "family mental disorders" occurred in 28 of 57 cases and were unrelated to prognosis. This included 24 cases of schizophrenia, 18 cases of suicide (diagnosis not specified), and 10 cases of endogenous depressive psychosis. It is not specified whether these are first- or second-degree relatives or whether one type of disorder clustered in certain families. There is evidently an increased incidence of schizophrenia in the relatives, but neither the number of patients nor the percentage of first-degree relatives manifesting schizophrenia is reported. The increased incidence of depressive psychosis in some relatives suggests that some cases of infantile schizophrenia in this sample may have had psychotic forms of major affective disorder.

Kolvin (1971b) and Kallman and Roth (1956) reported data on family history. Kolvin reported that the parental schizophrenia rate was 9.4 percent (11.7 percent corrected for age), and Kallman and Roth reported 8.8 percent parental schizophrenia (12.5 percent corrected). These latter rates are close to age-corrected rates reported for adult schizophrenics (Slater and Cowie 1971): 4.4 percent (5.5 percent if probable cases are included). The higher rates in the childhood sample could reflect many factors, including higher genetic load in early-onset cases, as well as sampling and definitional factors. Kallman and Roth did not find increased incidence of affective symptoms or disorders in their sample, though Kolvin (1971c) did find that 23 percent of the parents of his patients had "depressive/neurotic disorder," defined very broadly. The composition of this group was acknowledged by Kolvin to be uncertain: "Precise diagnoses and reliable details were not readily available" (p. 400). The possibility exists that some parents, possibly similarly to Eggers's sample, had major affective disorders, possibly reflecting diagnostic heterogeneity in the LOP group.

The family incidence of mental illness data (Tsuang 1979) thus do tend to validate the diagnosis of LOP as a variant of schizophrenia in at least a subgroup of the LOP children. However, the possibility exists that some children were diagnosed as schizophrenic who in fact may have deserved other diagnoses, including psychotic forms of major affective disorder. All these studies were performed at times when major affective disorders were not believed to occur in childhood. Several diagnostic entities, psychotic and nonpsychotic, other than schizophrenia, most notably affective disorders, should be systematically assessed in relatives using modern assessment instruments (Endicott and Spitzer 1978) and diagnostic criteria (American Psychiatric Association 1980) in future studies.

CONCLUSIONS

We can thus draw the following conclusions regarding the diagnostic importance of hallucinations in children and adolescents:

1. There is some evidence that children (and adolescents to a lesser degree) may be predisposed to report the experience of hallucinations to a greater extent than adults. This may be a result of several factors: immature development of a consensual (versus egocentric) frame of reference, language, reality sense, and psychosocial autonomy. All of these factors make it more likely that children will hallucinate when under stress. This stress might be adverse social experiences or an episode of psychiatric disorder. Thus, hallucinations in children probably have less serious psychopathological import than hallucinations in adults.
2. It is likely that a sharp distinction cannot be made between "psychotic" and "normal" thinking in children, that there is a wide phenomenological "gray area."
3. The application *childhood schizophrenia* is an outmoded concept. Childhood psychoses can be subdivided by a number of parameters into at least two distinct subgroups.

The late-onset group of childhood psychoses (LOP), with onset of psychosis above five years of age, show a high incidence of hallucinations and delusions and have been described as early-onset forms of schizophrenia. There is, however, evidence from phenomenology, follow-up data, and family incidence of mental illness that this may be a heterogeneous group of conditions. It is particularly possible that LOP may include psychotic forms of affective disorder, but other Axis One disorders may be represented as well. The clarification of these issues awaits future research.

References

American Psychiatric Association: Diagnostic and Statistical Manual of Mental Disorders (Second Edition). Washington, DC, American Psychiatric Association, 1968

American Psychiatric Association: Diagnostic and Statistical Manual of Mental Disorders (Third Edition). Washington, DC, American Psychiatric Association, 1980

Annell AL: The prognosis of psychotic conditions of childhood. Acta Psychiatr Scand 39:235–297, 1963

Asarnow RF, Sherman T: Studies of visual information processing in schizophrenic children. Child Dev 55:249–261, 1984

Astrachan B, Harrow M, Braver D, et al: A checklist for the diagnosis of schizophrenia. Brit J Psychiatry 121:525–539, 1972

Baker M, Dorzab J, Winokur G, et al: Depressive disease: classification and clinical characteristics. Compr Psychiatry 12:354–365, 1971

Bender L: Schizophrenia in childhood. The Nervous Child 1:138–140, 1942

Bender L: Childhood schiophrenia: clinical study of one hundred schizophrenic children. Am J Orthopsychiatry 17:40–56, 1947

Bender L: Childhood schizophrenia. Psychiatr 27:663–681, 1953

Bender L: The concept of pseudopsychopathic schizophrenia in adolescents. Am J Orthopsychiatry 29:491–512, 1959

Bender L: The life course of schizophrenic children. Biol Psychiatry 2:165–172, 1970

Bender L: Alpha and omega of childhood schizophrenia. Journal of Autism and Childhood Schizophrenia 1:115–118, 1971

Bender L: The family patterns of 100 schizophrenic children observed at Bellevue, 1935–1952. Journal of Autism and Childhood Schizophrenia 4:279–292, 1974

Bender L: Schizophrenic spectrum disorders in the families of schizophrenic children, in Genetic Research in Psychiatry. Edited by Fieve RR, Rosenthal D, Brill H. Baltimore, Johns Hopkins University Press, 1975

Bender L, Lipkowitz HH: Hallucinations in children. Am J Orthopsychiatry 10:471–490, 1940

Bender L, Vogel BF: Imaginary companions in children. Am J Orthopsychiatry 11:56–65, 1941

Bender L, Grugett AE: A study of certain epidemiological problems in a group of children with childhood schizophrenia. Am J Orthopsychiatry 26:131–145, 1956

Bender L, Freedman AM, Grugett AE, et al: Schizophrenia in childhood—a confirmation of the diagnosis. Proceedings of the American Neurological Association 77:67–73, 1952

Bleuler E: Dementia Praecox or the Group of the Schizophrenias. New York, International Universities Press, 1950

Burke P, Del Beccaro M, McCauley E, et al: Hallucinations in children. J Am Acad Child Psychiatry 24:71–75, 1985

Canino I, Bird H: The social psychiatry of espiritismo. Findings of a study in a psychiatric population of Puerto Ricans and other Hispanics. J Am Acad Child Psychiatry 20:725–740, 1981

Cantor S, Pearce J, Pezzot-Pearce T, et al: The group of hypotonic schizophrenics. Schizophr Bull 7:1–11, 1981

Cantor S, Trevenen R, Postuma R: Muscle biopsy in hypotonic schizophrenic children: a preliminary report. Schizophr Bull 5:616–622, 1979

Cantor S, Trevenen C, Postuma R, et al: Is childhood schizophrenia a cholinergic disease? I. muscle morphology. Arch Gen Psychiatry 37:658–667, 1980

Carlson G, Strober M: Manic–depressive illness in early adolescence. J Am Acad Child Psychiatry 17:138–153, 1978

Carpenter WT, Strauss JS, Bartko JJ: Flexible system for the diagnosis of schizophrenia: report from the WHO pilot study of schizophrenia. Science 182:1275–1278, 1973

Chambers WJ, Puig-Antich J, Tabrizi MA, et al: Psychotic symptoms in prepubertal major depressive disorder. Arch Gen Psychiatry 39:921–927, 1982

Chambers WJ, Puig-Antich J, Hirsch M, et al: The assessment of affective disorders in children and adolescents by semistructured interview. Arch Gen Psychiatry, in press

Chapman LJ: Recent advances in the study of schizophrenic cognition. Schizophr Bull 5:568–580, 1979

Chapman LJ, Chapman JP: Scales for rating psychotic and psychotic-like experiences as continua. Schizophr Bull 6:476–489, 1980

de Sanctis S: On some varieties of daementia praecox (translation of 1906 original), in Modern Perspectives in International Child Psychiatry. Edited by Howells JG, translated by Osborn ML. Edinburgh: Oliver & Boyd, 1969, pp 590–609

Despert JL: A comparative study of thinking in schizophrenic children and in children of preschool age. Am J Psychiatry 97:189, 1940

Despert JL: Delusional and hallucinatory experiences in children. Am J Psychiatry 104:528–537, 1948

Egdell HG, Kolvin I: Childhood hallucinations. J Child Psychol Psychiatry 13:279–287, 1972

Eggers C: Verlaufsweisen Kindlicher und Prapuberalle Schizophrenien. Berlin, Springer-Verlag, 1973

Eggers C: Course and prognosis of childhood schizophrenia. Journal of Autism and Childhood Schizophrenia 8:21–36, 1978

Eisenberg L: The course of childhood schizophrenia. AMA Archives of Neurology and Psychiatry 78:69–83, 1957

Eisenberg L: Hallucinations in children, in Hallucinations. Edited by West LJ. New York, Grune & Stratton, 1962

Endicott J, Spitzer, RL: A diagnostic interview. Arch Gen Psychiatry 35:837, 1978

Feighner JP, Robins E, Guze SB, et al: Diagnostic criteria for use in psychiatric research. Arch Gen Psychiatry 26:57–63, 1972

Foley MA, Johnson MK, Raye CL: Age-related changes in confusion between memories for thoughts and memories for speech. Child Dev 54:51–60, 1983

Freeman LN, Poznanski EO, Grossman J, et al: Psychotic and depressed children: a new entity. J Am Acad Child Psychiatry 24:95–102, 1985

Green WH, Campbell M, Hardesty AS: A comparison of schizophrenic and autistic children. J Am Acad Child Psychiatry 23:399–409, 1984

Gruber HE, Voneche JJ: The Essential Piaget. New York, Basic Books, 1977

Howells JG, Giurguis WR: Childhood schizophrenia 20 years later. Arch Gen Psychiatry 41:123–128, 1984

Hollingshead AB, Redlich FC: Social Class and Mental Illness. New York, Wiley, 1958

Inhelder B, Piaget J: The Growth of Logical Thinking From Childhood to Adolescence. New York, Basic Books, 1958

Jaspers K: Zur Analyse der Trugwahrnehmungen (Leibhaftigkeit und Realitätsurteil), in Gesammelte Schriften zur Psychopathologie. Edited by Jaspers K. Berlin, Springer, 1963a

Jaspers K: Die Trugwahrnehmungen, in Gesammelte Schriften zur Psychopathologie. Edited by Jaspers K. Berlin, Springer, 1963b

Johnson MK, Raye CL: Reality monitoring. Psychol Rev 88:67–85, 1981

Kallman FJ, Roth B: Genetic aspects of preadolescent schizophrenia. Am J Psychiatry 112:599–606, 1956

Koehler K: First rank symptoms of schizophrenia: questions concerning clinical boundaries. Brit J Psychiatry 134:236-248, 1979

Kolvin I: Studies in the childhood psychoses. I. diagnostic criteria and classification. Brit J Psychiatry 118:381-384, 1971

Kolvin I, Ounsted C, Humphrey M, et al: Studies in the childhood psychoses. II. the phenomenology of childhood psychoses. Brit J Psychiatry 118:385-395, 1971a

Kolvin I, Ounsted C, Richardson LM, et al: Studies in the childhood psychoses. III. the family and social background of childhood psychoses. Brit J Psychiatry 118:396-402, 1971b

Kolvin I, Garside RF, Kidd JSH: Studies in the childhood psychoses. IV. parental personality and attitude and childhood psychoses. Brit J Psychiatry 118:403-406, 1971c

Kolvin I, Ounsted C, Roth M: Studies in the childhood psychoses. V. cerebral dysfunction and childhood psychoses. Brit J Psychiatry 118:407-414, 1971d

Kolvin I, Humphrey M, McNay A: Studies in the childhood psychoses. VI. cognitive factors in childhood psychoses. Brit J Psychiatry 118:415-419, 1971e

Makita K: The age of onset of childhood schizophrenia. Folia Psychiatr Neurol Jpn 20:111-121, 1966

Mussen P, Conger J, Kagan J: Child Development and Personality (Fifth edition). New York, Harper & Row, 1979

Neuchterlein KH, Dawson ME: Informational processing and attentional functioning in the developmental course of schizophrenic disorders. Schizophr Bull 10:160-203, 1984a

Neuchterlein KH, Dawson ME: A neuristic vulnerability/stress model of schizophrenic episodes. Schizophr Bull 10:300-312, 1984b

Parnas J, Schulsinger F, Schulsinger H, et al: Behavioral precursors of schizophrenia spectrum. Arch Gen Psychiatry 39:658–664, 1982

Petty LK, Ornitz EM, Michelman JD, et al: Autistic children who become schizophrenic. Arch Gen Psychiatry 41:129–135, 1984

Puig-Antich J, Gittelman R: Depression in childhood and adolescence, in Handbook of Affective Disorders. Edited by Paykel E. New York, Guilford, 1982

Puig-Antich J, Chambers WJ, Tabrizi MA: The clinical assessment of current depressive episodes in children: interviews with parents and children, in Childhood Depression. Edited by Cantwell D and Carlson G. New York, Spectrum, 1983

Puig-Antich J, Perel JM, Lupatkin W, et al: Imipramine effectiveness in prepubertal major depressive disorders. I. plasma level relationship to clinical response of the depressive syndrome. Arch Gen Psychiatry, in press

Rutschmann J, Cornblatt B, Erlenmeyer-Kimling L: Sustained attention in children at risk for schizophrenia. Arch Gen Psychiatry 34:571–575, 1977

Rutter M: The development of infantile autism. Psychol Med 4:147–163, 1974

Rutter M, Shaffer D, Shepherd M: An evaluation of the proposal for a multiaxial classification of child psychiatric disorders. Psychol Med 3:244–250, 1973

Schneider K: Clinical Psychopathology. New York, Grune & Stratton, 1959

Slater E, Cowie V: The Genetics of Mental Disorders. Oxford University Press, London, 1971

Spitzer RL, Endicott J, Robins E: Research diagnostic criteria. rationale and reliability. Arch Gen Psychiatry 35:773–782, 1978

Strauss JS: Hallucinations and delusions as points on continua function. Arch Gen Psychiatry 21:581, 1969

Strauss JS, Carpenter WT: Prediction of outcome in schizophrenia. I. Characteristics of outcome. Arch Gen Psychiatry 27:739–746, 1972

Strober M, Green J, Carlson G: Phenomenology and subtypes of major depressive disorder in adolescence. J Affective Disord 3:281–290, 1981

Tsuang MT: Schizoaffective disorder. Arch Gen Psychiatry 36:633–634, 1979

Vaillant GE: A ten year follow up of remitting schizophrenics. Schizophr Bull 4:78–85, 1978

Vrono MS: Schizophrenia in childhood and adolescence. International Journal of Mental Health 2:8–11, 1973/1974

Werry JS: The childhood psychoses, in Psychopathological Disorders of Childhood. Edited by Quay H and Werry JS. New York, John Wiley & Sons, 1979

Wilking V, Paoli C: The hallucinatory experience. J Am Acad Child Psychiatry 5:431–440, 1966

Williams JBW: The multiaxial system of D.S.M. III, I. its origin and critiques. Arch Gen Psychiatry 42:175–180, 1985

Wing JK, Cooper JE, Sartorius N: The Measurement and Classification of Psychiatric Symptoms. London, Cambridge University Press, 1974

World Health Organization: The International Pilot Study of Schizophrenia, vol 1. Geneva, World Health Organization, 1973

World Health Organization: Schizophrenia. An International Follow-Up Study. New York, Wiley, 1979

Hallucinations: Biological and Cognitive Mechanisms

Sidney Katz, M.D.
Mark Press, M.H.L.
Lenore Engel, M.D.

4

Hallucinations: Biological and Cognitive Mechanisms

For the purposes of this chapter, hallucinations may be defined as in the *Diagnostic and Statistical Manual of Mental Disorders, Third Edition (DSM-III;* American Psychiatric Association 1980): a sensory perception without external stimulation of the relevant sensory organ. Hallucinations have an immediate sense of reality, even though in some cases the subject is cognitively aware that this is not so. Discussion of the issues in defining hallucinations is beyond the scope of this chapter.

We intend to cover the neurophysiological and neurochemical investigations of hallucinatory states. We will examine dream states, drug-induced hallucinations, amphetamine psychoses, and hallucinatory experiences in some nonfunctional illnesses. Particular emphasis will be placed on the role of serotonin and its interaction with other neurotransmitters. We will also briefly review some theories of the cognitive and perceptual mechanisms underlying hallucinations.

Because of the difficulty of directly studying so subjective an experience as a hallucination, attempts have been made to use dream states and drug-induced experiences as models. Similarities between dreams and madness have been recognized throughout the ages and evoked comment from, among others, Plato, Aristotle, Kant, and Freud. Kant (Fischman 1983) referred to the lunatic as a "wakeful dreamer." Jacques Moreau de Tours (Fischman 1983) in the mid-1800s, after experiencing the effects of hashish, compared the experience to a sleepless dream and noted the similarities between dreams, drug-induced states, and psychosis. All three states share the phenomenon of vivid sensory experiences in the absence of, or with limited, external sensory stimulation and with strong affective components. Only work with adults is discussed in all the literature to which we refer. We are unaware of any work in this area that deals specifically with children.

PHYSIOLOGICAL AND BIOCHEMICAL MECHANISMS

Many investigators used chemically induced psychoses to study mental illness. Knauer and Maloney (1913) were the first of many to use mescaline in this pursuit. Kluver (1928), probably the most prodigious researcher in this area, carefully described and categorized the various stages of hallucinatory experiences following mescaline ingestion.

In 1938, Hoffman (1979) serendipitously discovered lysergic acid diethylamide (LSD), which at one stage was regarded as a model for psychosis. This model was challenged by Hollister (1962, 1968) and others who felt that the two conditions were phenomenologically different. Their objections were that a) LSD hallucinations were primarily visual whereas those of schizophrenia were primarily auditory; b) in drug-induced states, language was reality related whereas in schizophrenia it was more disorganized and incoherent; c) schizophrenics withdraw socially whereas drug users do not; and d) drug users are usually euphoric whereas schizophrenics are anxious and distressed.

Hollister argued that, for the above reasons, drug states were not an appropriate model for the study of psychosis. These objections were reviewed by a number of authors, including Young (1974), who argued that the comparison between acute drug states and chronic schizophrenia as seen in the United States was inappropriate. If, instead, acute drug states were compared to acute schizophrenia, one found that a) visual hallucinations occurred equally frequently in both conditions; b) drug users were also inclined to withdraw socially, particularly if unaware of having been given the drug or in the later states of a drug experience; c) there was little difference in the coherence of language; and d) acute schizophrenics frequently showed euphoria in the initial stages of the illness and users of hallucinogens often experienced considerable distress. One may justifiably conclude, therefore, that there is sufficient similarity between drug states and acute schizophrenia to allow the former to be used as a model for the latter without implying an identity of the two conditions.

The major hallucinogenic drugs studies include LSD, psilocin, DMT (dimethyltryptamine), 5-methoxy-DMT, DOM (2,5-dimethoxy-4-methylamphetamine), and mescaline. Psilocin, LSD, DMT, and 5-methoxy-DMT all share the indole nucleus, which is also found in the neurotransmitter serotonin. This shared nucleus may be the basis for the hallucinogens' serotonergic inhibition. The phenethylamine hallucinogens do not share an indole nucleus. Nevertheless, they act as hallucinogens in different animal species, including humans, in a way similar to the indoleamines. They cause similar behavioral and perceptual changes, and they develop cross tolerance with the indoleamines. It is likely, therefore, that both classes of hallucinogens act through a common biological mechanism.

The drug LSD was found to be a powerful inhibitor of serotonin in vitro. In the early 1960s Freedman (1961) found that LSD increased the level of serotonin and decreased 5-HIAA (5-hydroxyindoleacetic acid), the major serotonin metabolite, in rat brain. This was understood to reflect the inhibition by LSD of neuronal release of serotonin. In the mid-1960s the serotonergic nuclei were identified and found to be located almost entirely in the raphe of the brain stem with widely distributed axons. The axons of the cells in the dorsal and medial raphe innervate the ventral lateral geniculate nucleus, the superior colliculus, and the limbic system (amygdala and hippocampus). These systems are involved in visual perception and in emotional response to information, two components of hallucinatory states.

Aghajanian et al. (1968) inserted microelectrodes into the serotonergic cells in the dorsal raphe in rats and measured the reduction in firing rate of these cells following intravenous administration of LSD. Adjacent nonserotonergic cells were unaffected. Introduction of LSD in minute amounts directly to the cells by means of microiontophoresis demonstrated that LSD affected the neuron directly. These studies appeared to confirm the role of LSD as an inhibitor of serotonergic function.

Jacobs and Trulson (1979) advanced the hypothesis that dreams, drug-induced hallucinations, and psychoses share the same biochemical mechanism. They proposed that all three occur by decreasing serotonergic activity at the raphe nucleus. These authors performed a series of elegant experiments on nonanesthetized cats in which they placed microelectrodes in awake, moving animals and recorded single neuron activity. In the awake condition, serotonergic neurons fire at a slow regular rate of 0.5–2 per minute. Firing rate increases with arousal and decreases in the quiet state, with further decreases in non-REM (rapid eye movement) sleep and almost no firing in REM sleep, that state in which most human dreaming occurs. With active awakening, firing rate increases more rapidly than in passive awakening and is uncorrelated with level of motor activity. Serotonergic cells are located in the most primitive part of the brain (which has changed little phylogenetically) and are among the first cells to be differentiated. The assumption is that these neurons' role is tonic modulating rather than processing or dynamic and that they are essential to the process of distinguishing internal from external information.

Trulson and Jacobs (1976) identified two behaviors in cats that occurred in response to single-dose administration of hallucinogens but not in response to saline or nonhallucinogenic psychoactive drugs. Responses were dose dependent. These behaviors were a) limb flicks, the raising and shaking of the paw normally done only in response to water or foreign bodies, and b) abortive grooming, where the cat begins to bite, lick, or scratch but fails to complete the action. The authors speculate that these abnormal acts occur as responses to hallucination-like phenomena. (The validity of this model will be touched on later in this chapter.)

Neuronal monitoring during the studies done with 5-methoxy-

DMT, a short-acting hallucinogen, indicated a marked suppression of neuronal firing, which correlated in time with the limb flicks and abortive grooming. Similar changes were observed with other hallucinogens. Two additional phenomena observed with LSD, however, indicated that the process was more complicated than the mere suppression of serotonergic activity. The behavioral effects of LSD lasted twice as long as did the suppression of serotonergic neuronal firing, and tolerance developed to the behavioral consequences even though suppression of serotonergic activity continued.

As with LSD and other hallucinogens, serotonin has been implicated in the production of hallucinations with amphetamines and methylphenidate. Previously, amphetamines' psychoactive effect had been thought to be due to its effect on catecholamines alone, effects that occur rapidly. More recent studies indicate that it is the chronic administration of amphetamines that leads both to the decrease of serotonin and 5-HIAA and to behavior suggestive of hallucinations. Trulson and Jacobs (1979b), in studies on cats, found that serotonin depletion coincided in time with the emergence of limb flicking and abortive grooming and that these effects did not appear before three days of amphetamine administration.

Clinical experience with human ingestion of amphetamines or methylphenidate indicated that hallucinatory experiences usually develop after prolonged ingestion of high doses. However, there are reports of hallucinations developing after periods as short as several days and at low doses. This suggests that hallucinations may also be mediated by neurotransmitters other than serotonin. It is possible that amphetamines may also act by direct effect on the noradrenergic neurons in the lateral geniculate nucleus (Young 1981). We have previously alluded to the similarity between dreams, drug states, and hallucinations and the role that serotonin is thought to play in those conditions. It appears that drugs involving serotonin also affect REM sleep, during which most dreams occur. Reserpine depletes serotonin and catecholamines and increases REM sleep, whereas monoamine oxidase (MAO) inhibitors increase serotonin and decrease REM sleep. Clomipramine blocks serotonin re-uptake (with little effect on norepinephrine) and reduces REM sleep. Narcolepsy, a disorder of REM sleep frequently accompanied by frightening hypnogogic hallucinations, can respond to clomipramine within 48 hours.

The hallucinogenic effects of LSD can be potentiated by drugs that decrease serotonin levels and reduced by drugs that increase available serotonin. Reserpine and PCPA (parachlorophenylalanine), which interfere with serotonin synthesis, act synergistically with LSD, as they do with other hallucinogens. Clomipramine and MAO inhibitors partly protect against hallucinations caused by LSD.

Both the serotonin and dopamine theories of psychosis and/or hallucinations appeared initially to be attractive, but significant questions have been raised about them in recent years. The attractiveness of the serotonin theory lies in the following findings:

1. Hallucinogens depress serotonergic neurons in the dorsal raphe without affecting adjacent nonserotonergic neurons.
2. A number of hallucinogens generate behaviors in animals that appear to parallel human hallucinations and that are correlated with depressed firing of serotonergic neurons. There is a dose–response relationship for both depressed firing and behaviors as well as a time relationship between depressed firing and these behaviors.
3. Serotonergic neurons inhibit their target cells, and their depression would lead to disinhibition of these target cells. The disinhibition of these cells leads, among other effects, to increased secretion of dopamine and may explain the role of serotonin in a dopamine theory of psychosis.

Unfortunately, other studies have failed to find a constant relationship between depression of serotonergic neurons and behavior. For example, Trulson and Jacobs (1979a) found that low doses of 5-methoxy-DMT produced limb flicking in the cat without depression of the dorsal raphe, whereas high doses could depress these neurons without accompanying limb flicking. With phenylethylamine hallucinogens (DOM, mescaline), the situation is even more complex. Moderate doses of DOM produce behavior change without raphe suppression, whereas high doses increase both deviant behavior and serotonergic firing. Mescaline affects behavior with no raphe changes. We have already noted that with LSD, tolerance develops for the behavioral effects despite ongoing suppression of the raphe nuclei and the behavioral effects outlast raphe suppression.

A number of other findings challenge the presynaptic explanation for the hallucinogenic effects of these drugs. Both 5-HT and L-tryptophan reduce raphe cell firing without producing behavioral or perceptual changes. Lisuride, a substance structurally related to LSD, produced both reduced raphe cell firing and behavioral changes in rats similar to those caused by LSD. Lisuride is not hallucinogenic in humans. The lisuride findings raise the question of whether limb flicks and abortive grooming are adequate measures of the hallucinogenic activity of these drugs. Nevertheless, these measures have been useful in elucidating the effects of LSD and other hallucinogens and in identifying some of the sites of their actions in the central nervous system. Other models will need to be developed that more closely reflect the hallucinogenic effect in humans.

Several explanations have been offered for these dissociations:

1. Subgroups of serotonergic raphe cells are differentially affected by these drugs. Trulson et al. (1981) indeed found that hallucinogens that previously had been described as depressing raphe neuron activity actually could exert an excitatory effect on a subset of these neurons.
2. The hallucinogens may have a direct effect on the serotonergic target cells in addition to their effect on the raphe cells.
3. At least in the case of LSD and DOM, there may be a direct effect on the dopaminergic and adrenergic systems in addition to the effect on the raphe cells.

The focus has been on the presynaptic effects of the hallucinogens. Recently there has been a shift to the role of the postsynaptic neurons in producing the behavioral and perceptual changes caused by the hallucinogens. Heyms et al. (1984) list a number of reasons for this change in focus:

1. The ^{3}H-LSD binding assays remain unchanged following the destruction of the 5-HT neurons. Bound LSD can be displaced by serotonin at the postsynaptic sites. This suggests that the binding of LSD is associated with serotonin receptors. The binding of LSD at presynaptic sites is not affected by serotonin.

2. With repeated use of LSD, the behavioral effects are no longer elicited, while suppression of raphe firing continues. There is, however, an accompanying decrease in the number of available postsynaptic serotonergic binding sites. The consequent change in sensitivity of the postsynaptic neuron may explain the dissociation between raphe neuron activity and behavioral changes.

3. Serotonin depletion prior to the administration of LSD enhances the behavioral effects of the hallucinogen, suggesting increased postsynaptic sensitivity to the drug.

4. In rats serotonin antagonists can block the behavioral effects of hallucinogens without changing the presynaptic firing rates.

5. Monoamine oxidase inhibitors can block the behavioral effects of LSD in humans, rats, and cats; MAO inhibitors increase serotonin availability and thus reduce the available binding sites for LSD.

Nelson (1982) described a number of different serotonergic binding sites. Using the ligand-binding technique, he was able to identify at least two different types of binding sites. The first, with a high affinity for ^{3}H-serotonin, are referred to as 5-HT$_1$ binding sites. The second type of binding site, 5-HT$_2$, has a high affinity for ^{3}H-spiperone and is mainly located in the frontal cortex. The serotonin antagonists referred to above seem to be more potent at the 5-HT$_2$ receptors.

Heym et al. (1984) investigated the effects of serotonin antagonists on the action of hallucinogens. They administered mianserin (a serotonin antagonist) to cats 30 minutes before giving the hallucinogens. The behavioral effects of the hallucinogens were blocked by this procedure. The presynaptic effect—that is, decreased firing of the 5-HT neurons—was unaffected. Mianserin pretreatment did not affect the alertness or general motor activity of the cats. Pretreatment with mianserin did not eliminate the behavioral effects of the nonhallucinogens lisuride and apomorphine. Dopamine antagonists given prior to the administration of the hallucinogens did not affect behavior or the rate of raphe neuron firing.

Mianserin acts mainly at the postsynaptic $5\text{-}HT_2$ receptor sites. Heym et al. (1984), following these studies, concluded that the effect of hallucinogens on the $5\text{-}HT_2$ binding sites is critical for the production of the behavioral and perceptual effects of these drugs. They suggest that the presynaptic effects are insignificant or contribute only in a small way to this mechanism.

The dopaminergic model of psychosis is also questionable. It is clear that amphetamine psychoses generally occur only after sustained administration of the drug whereas dopamine changes occur immediately after single doses. Alpert and Friedhoff (1980) suggested that the timing of the amphetamine psychoses coincides more closely with dopamine depletion than with its increased availability. Animal studies show that by the time hallucination-like behaviors emerge after continued amphetamine administration, there is also a reduction of serotonin and 5-HIAA.

It is possible that the hallucinogens also affect the noradrenergic system. McCall and Aghajanian (1980) reported that LSD and related hallucinogens sensitize serotonin and norepinephrine receptors on motor neurons in the facial nucleus. This raises the possibility that the hallucinogens may sensitize the sensory neurons and contribute to the psychedelic activity of these drugs.

Commisaris and Davis (1982) described the effects of DMT and 5-MeODMT on the acoustic startle response in rats. Systemic administration of these two hallucinogens resulted in a reduction of the response with DMT and an increase of the response with 5-MeODMT. When these two drugs were injected into the lateral ventricle, they were equipotent in depressing the response. When both hallucinogens were injected into the subarachnoid space of the spine, 5-MeODMT increased the startle response but DMT had no effect. It is clear that a) the same hallucinogen can have different effects on different parts of the nervous system and b) different hallucinogens may have differing effects on the same parts of the nervous system. This may in part explain some of the contradictory findings in studies using different hallucinogens.

From the preceding review, it is clear that serotonin plays a significant role in producing the effects of hallucinogenic agents. It has been the major neurotransmitter studied to date, although not the only one. Both presynaptic and postsynaptic sites of action have been postulated to account for the behavioral and perceptual effects of hallucinogens, with new evidence focusing on the importance of the postsynaptic site. Despite the heavy weight of reviews on serotonin's role, it is unreasonable to suggest that only a single neurotransmitter system is responsible for hallucinatory phenomena. A role for both dopamine and serotonin has already been described. In addition, Domino and Ruffing (1982) suggest a role for the opioid receptor in the behavioral response to hallucinogens. Opioid antagonists can potentiate the behavioral effect of both DMT and LSD in rats. Although LSD and DMT can cause many similar responses in animals and humans, their interactions with some agonists and antagonists do differ. This suggests that in addition to common biological pathways, they also have specific and distinct actions.

Another area of neurochemical investigation has been the relation of MAO to hallucinatory phenomena. Studies have noted an association between low platelet MAO activity and hallucinations in schizophrenics but no such association in affective psychotics (Meltzer et al. 1980). It is unclear to what extent platelet MAO activity is related to MAO activity in the brain. Two types of MAO, A and B, exist. Human platelet MAO is type B, whereas both types are found in the central nervous system. Low platelet MAO has also been reported in alcoholics and social extroverts and would thus appear to be a finding with nonspecific psychiatric implications.

Brandys and Yehuda (1983) suggested that LSD and other hallucinogens act as dopamine agonists. They argue that the hallucinogens have an inhibitory effect on the MAOs. This action, together with the serotonergic actions of the hallucinogens, explains the contradictory findings discussed above. The discussion is purely speculative, and no firm evidence is offered.

PSYCHOLOGICAL MECHANISMS

Psychological aspects of the hallucinatory process that require analysis include a) the factors underlying the general hallucinatory experience, b) variables that determine individual differences in this process, and c) the determinants of specific hallucinatory content. We will concentrate on the first two elements, content being heavily determined by emotional and dynamic issues discussed elsewhere in this monograph, and deal with a few theories of current significance, some of their common elements, and the evidence for or against their validity.

West (1962) has elaborated a perceptual release theory based on the original work of Hughlings Jackson, founded on the following assumptions:

1. Life experiences affect the brain so as to leave permanent neural traces that are the basis for thought, memory, and imagination.
2. Personality is best understood as the interplay of internal and external forces in which the neural traces are constantly interwoven into images, fantasies, dreams, and thoughts.
3. A constant scanning and screening process determines what will be allowed to enter the field of conscious awareness. The organization of this scanning–screening process is dependent on an optimal input of external stimulation.

If effective environmental sensory input is diminished, while at the same time an adequate arousal level for awareness is maintained, previously recorded percepts can then emerge into awareness and may be experienced as externally real. West notes that effective external sensory input can be reduced in three ways: a) absolute decrease of stimulation (for example, sensory deprivation); b) input overload (for example, great emotional disturbance, delirium); and c) decreased psychological contact with the environment (for example, dissociation, toxic states).

According to West, a passive receipt of sufficient external stimulation will prevent the appearance of hallucinations. Fischer (1970) redefined hallucinations as "intensely active sensations with blocked peripheral voluntary motor manifestation" (p 304). Experiences can thus be categorized in terms of a ratio of sensory stimulation to motor activity (S/M) in which heightening sensory awareness or reducing voluntary motor activity can lead to a hallucination. Motor verification is necessary to constrain the information in a system; in its absence, previous traces reappear and may be experienced as real.

Fischer cites evidence for his theory from neurophysiological states with a high S/M ratio that are hallucinatory. These include drug states, in which inhibition of motor activity was first noted by Rothlin (1957), and REM sleep states, in which heightened dreaming is accompanied by motor inhibition. He also adduces evidence for his position from studies describing patients immobilized in body casts, traction, or tank-type respirators in which hallucinations have been reported. Fischer thus concludes that motor activity, rather than mere external sensory stimulation, is necessary to counteract hallucinations. This position is in contrast to West's. Margo et al. (1981) did in fact find that requiring the subject to give an overt response to auditory stimuli inhibited hallucinations.

Slade (1976b) hypothesized a four-factor theory of auditory hallucinations with the following elements:

1. Psychological stress engenders a disturbance of mood state and a condition of internal emotional arousal.
2. Internal arousal interacts with the second factor, hallucinatory predisposition level. If this interaction raises the hallucinatory tendency above a specific threshold, hallucinations may result, dependent on the third factor.
3. The third factor, level of external stimulation, will then determine whether the subject consciously experiences a hallucination. Consciousness is a channel of limited capacity, and external and internal stimulation are constantly competing for the focus of conscious response.
4. The fourth factor hypothesized is a subsequent improvement of mood state as a consequence of the hallucination (a difficult hypothesis to accept in the face of clinical experience). This

mood improvement acts as a reinforcement and may lower the critical threshold for an individual to hallucinate. This in turn would allow the subject to hallucinate more readily in the future in response to weaker stresses.

Slade's model is clearly the most complex of those proposed, involving interaction of constitutional, environmental, and experiential dimensions. Evidence for its various elements is uneven. Although stress events do seem related to the occurrence of psychosis, it is not clear that they are specifically related to the onset of hallucinations, though this is not an unreasonable assumption. Slade himself cited the work of Alpert et al. (1970) and Allen and Agus (1968), both of whom found that hallucinations could be induced in patients with hallucinatory histories by increasing physiological arousal.

Further evidence suggesting the relation of internal physiological arousal and hallucinations was reported by Cooklin et al. (1983). They studied spontaneous fluctuations in skin conductance, an index of autonomic arousal, in schizophrenics during hallucinatory and nonhallucinatory periods and found a clear association between the onset of hallucinations and a rise in spontaneous fluctuation rate. The authors themselves reported uncertainty as to whether arousal predisposes one to hallucinations or hallucinatory experiences increase arousal. They had included an experimental manipulation to address this question, which was unsuccessful. Nonetheless, they did find that the amount of hallucinatory activity changed significantly, independently of the spontaneous fluctuation rate, suggesting that arousal was not a direct consequence of schizophrenic pathology and indirectly supporting the role of arousal in predisposing one to hallucinatory activity.

More evidence exists for elements of the second factor, the predisposition to hallucinate. Both Mintz and Alpert (1972) and Slade (1976a, 1976b) found results suggesting that a combination of a tendency toward vivid auditory imagery and impaired reality testing in the auditory mode potentiated hallucinations. Other investigations (Heilbrun et al. 1983) have found, however, that vividness of imagery does not differentiate hallucinators and that in at least some cases these individuals have less vivid imagery. Brett and Starker (1977) found that neither vividness of mental imagery nor spontaneous imagery in daydreams differentiated hallucinating schizophrenics from nonhallucinating schizophrenics or medical patients. A similar failure to find vividness of imagery differences between hallucinating and nonhallucinating schizophrenics was reported by Catts et al. (1980). The weight of present evidence thus indicates that vividness of imagery is unrelated to hallucinatory predisposition and is an unproductive research path to follow.

Mintz and Alpert's (1972) other suggestion has been more fruitful. Several studies have pointed to an impaired ability to confidently and accurately identify neutral realities as being related to hallucinations. Evidence exists that even nonpsychiatric subjects can under particular conditions have difficulty distinguishing the real from the imaginary (Johnson and Raye 1981; Posey and Losch 1983; Spanos and Stam 1979). Heilbrun et al.'s (1983) finding that hallucinating process schizophrenics are deficient in localizing sounds in space also supports the notion that impairments in cognitive processes of reality interpretation underlie hallucinations.

Bentall and Slade (1985) reported a pair of experiments further supporting a relationship between the cognitive ability to assess reality and hallucinatory experience. Normal subjects were separated into high and low scorers on the Launay–Slade Hallucination Scale (LSHS; Launay and Slade 1981). Schizophrenics were separated into hallucinators and nonhallucinators. They then were presented with a signal detection test in which they had to listen to a tape of white noise, within which a real word was embedded. Subjects were asked to report when they heard the voice and with what degree of confidence. All groups of subjects, both normal and schizophrenic, were equivalent in sensitivity to the detection of a real stimulus. However, both high-LSHS normals and hallucinating patients were more likely to incorrectly report that they heard a voice when none had been presented. Hallucinators are thus shown to have a greater tendency to believe under some conditions that stimuli are real even when they are not.

Heilbrun and Blum (1984) offered further evidence that the hallucinatory predisposition entails various cognitive skills or deficits. In a study of hallucinating and nonhallucinating reactive and process psychiatric patients, they found reactive hallucinators to be more intolerant of ambiguity than were the nonhallucinators. The reactive hallucinators also made more errors than any other groups on the task requiring word identification in the presence of distracting stimuli. Hallucinators were also less able to generate alternative and unusual word meanings than were nonhallucinators. Heilbrun and Blum's (1984) overall conclusion was that "particular cognitive attributes, probably acting in concert, place the individual at risk for auditory hallucinations" (p 511).

Indirect support of developmental–cognitive factors as a component of the predisposition to hallucinate is offered by the work of Garralda (1984a, 1984b, 1984c) and Zigler (1983). In a study of nonpsychotic children with hallucinations, Garralda (1984a, 1984b) described a strong association between marked verbal performance discrepancies on an intelligence test and hallucinations. Other factors such as vividness of imagination, daydreaming, and inadequate social stimulation failed to differentiate hallucinators from controls. His data also suggest a developmental role in the perceived location of the hallucinations, being seen primarily in internal space below the age of 13 and externally afterward. These hallucinations were not prodromal psychotic states, for in a follow-up Garralda (1984b) found no differences in diagnosis in adulthood between the childhood hallucinators and the controls. Garralda (1984c) also found an association between reading difficulties and hallucinations in a group of psychotic children, further suggesting a relation between cognitive deficits and hallucinations.

Zigler (1983) reported on a sample of paranoid and nonparanoid schizophrenics who were rated on the Social Competence Index, an instrument shown to correlate well with developmental levels. He hypothesized that delusional psychotics were at a higher level than hallucinators, and the results confirmed the expectation. A group of patients who had both hallucinations and delusions were intermediate in their development level. This latter finding refutes the notion that the hallucinators' lower developmental stage is a function of the severity of their pathology, indicating instead that lower levels of development are more likely to predispose to hallucinations rather than delusions.

Some evidence exists for the role of the third factor, the level of external stimulation, in hallucinations. In the volume edited by West (1962), various contributors discuss the facilitation of hallucinations under conditions of sensory deprivation. Feder (1982) reported a case in which auditory stimulation reduced hallucinations in a clinical patient. Margo et al. (1981) investigated the role of level of structure in auditory input (speech, music, white noise) and its attention-engaging properties (for example, interesting speech versus boring speech). Active monitoring (being asked to attend carefully to a passage so it could be retold) resulted in the greatest decrease in hallucinations. In passive listening, hallucinations were reduced as a function of the meaningfulness and attention-commanding properties of the stimuli. Contrary to West, variety in the external stimulus did not appear to be important in inhibiting hallucinations.

No significant investigations have yet been made of Slade's proposed fourth factor, the reduction of hallucinatory thresholds by reinforcement.

Horowitz (1970, 1975) has proposed a cognitive model of hallucinations incorporating four factors. The model is based on a definition of hallucinations as "mental experiences" that a) "occur in the form of images," b) "are derived from internal sources of information," c) "are appraised incorrectly as if from external sources of information," and d) "usually occur intrusively" (1975, p 789).

Each of these definitional elements refers to a discrete set of psychological processes, though together they form a unitary experience. The first emphasizes that the raw psychological data of hallucinations are images rather than encoded motor or lexical–verbal elements. Images are complex informational sets involving combinations of perception, memory, thought, and fantasy, whereas pure lexical thought would be unaccompanied either by action (for example, subvocal speech) or images (for example, no auditory or visual correlates). Horowitz noted that few lexical experiences are pure but, rather, that they vary in the degree of associated representations.

The second element emphasizes the constant balance of internal and external input in the formation of images. The third element focuses on an impairment of information processing that allows a vivid image to be perceived as external rather than internal. Such impairment can occur either as a consequence of brain dysfunction, such as toxic states, or of psychological processes, primarily defensive. A defense mechanism may operate by restricting the integration of related informational elements, allowing an image to be experienced as strange, external, or uninterpretable.

The final element emphasizes the intrusive and uncontrolled entry of the percept into conscious awareness, primarily because of emotional stress. These stresses may be a consequence of the nature of the perception itself, the emotional impact being so great as to make it difficult for the experience to be fully interpreted, or of eruptions of usually hidden feelings. One must remember that stress also affects the accuracy of processing in the third factor.

Aside from his own work, Horowitz's model has engendered little specific research testing. However, the work cited above suggests that vivid imagery is not a major element in the tendency to hallucinate, thus refuting Horowitz's first point.

All the psychological theories have basic common elements. They agree on the role of a) a balance of internal and external sources of information in either causing or permitting hallucinatory experiences, though disagreeing on the specific mechanism; b) psychological stress in creating conditions conducive to hallucinations, though again with disagreement as to the precise mechanism; and c) a cognitive deficit that interferes with the accurate interpretation of experience, above and beyond the contribution of affectual determinants.

SUMMARY

In this discussion of possible hallucinatory mechanisms, relationships between the biological and psychological theories are suggested. Most important is an apparent gating mechanism that regulates the quantity and intensity of external information to be admitted and the balance between internal and external stimulation to be attended to at any given time. This mechanism may be suspended physiologically, as in sleep, or pathologically, as in drug states or psychoses. It may also be suspended in such nonpathological phenomena as daydreaming and eidetic imagery.

This gating mechanism may function in several different ways. It regulates the entry of internal and external information into the processing system and determines the balance between them. Even when the organism is focused mainly on internal stimuli, the gating mechanism determines whether sufficient external information is admitted in order to allow distinction between real and imagined percepts. Where sufficient external information is not admitted, either because of a defect in the mechanism or a lack of external stimulation, internal stimuli may be perceived as hallucinations.

The studies cited here suggest that the serotonergic system is central to this gating mechanism. The action of serotonin at the raphe nuclei was initially considered central to this process. Recent work strongly indicates that the hallucinogen effect on the postsynaptic 5-HT_2 site is of greater consequence and the role of the raphe nuclei is uncertain. It is probable that other neurotransmitters also play a role in this regard, but this role has been less well researched.

A further issue considered is the relative salience of internal and external information. Clearly, one of the most important elements in determining salience is the emotional weight attached to the stimuli and their sources. It is also suggested by some authors that there are individual cognitive predispositions to place greater weight on certain types of information than on others. This includes preferences for specific perceptual channels such as the visual or auditory. One may speculate that highly salient internal information may reduce the impact of external information through the gating mechanisms and thus produce a hallucination.

Focus has shifted from the presynaptic serotonin neurons to the postsynaptic 5-HT_2 binding sites. It may well be that at this level the mechanism of producing hallucinations may not be by way of a gating mechanism alone but also of an increased stimulation of the postsynaptic target cells.

We do not suggest that the gating mechanism is necessarily implicated in all hallucinations. Information is processed at many cortical levels, and distortions or misperceptions at these levels may also result in a hallucinatory experience. Disruption at any level of central nervous system function, whether by structural or neurochemical alteration, can also produce hallucinations. The concepts outlined here are broad, but we believe they are useful in understanding hallucinations and in planning future research.

References

Aghajanian G, Foote WE, Sheard MH: Lysergic acid diethylamide sensitive neuronal units in the midbrain raphe. Science, 161:706–708, 1968

Allen TE, Agus B: Hyperventilation leading to hallucinations. Am J Psychiatry 125:632–637, 1968

Alpert M, Friedhoff AJ: An undopamine hypothesis of schizophrenia. Schizophr Bull 6:387–392, 1980

Alpert M, Angrist B, Diamond F, et al: Comparison of Ditran intoxication and acute alcohol psychoses, in Origin and Mechanisms of Hallucinations. Edited by Keup W. New York, Plenum, 1970, 245–259.

American Psychiatric Association: Diagnostic and Statistical Manual of Mental Disorders, 3rd ed. Washington, DC, American Psychiatric Association, 1980

Bentall RP, Slade PD: Reality testing and auditory hallucinations: a signal detection analysis. British Journal of Clinical Psychology 24:159–169, 1985

Brandys Y, Yehuda S: Indolamine hallucinogens as MAO inhibitor agents—a theoretical approach. Int J Neurosci 21:251–256, 1983

Brett EA, Starker S: Auditory imagery and hallucinations. J Nerv Ment Dis 164:394–400, 1977

Catts SV, Armstrong MS, Norcross K, et al: Auditory hallucinations and the verbal transformation effect. Psychol Med 10:139–144, 1980

Commisaris RL, Davis M: Opposite effects of n,n-dimethyltryptamin (DMT) and 5-methoxy-n,n-dimethyltryptamin (5MeODMzT) on acoustic startle: spinal versus brain sites of action. Neurosci Biobehav Rev 6:515–520, 1982

Cooklin R, Sturgeon D, Leff J: The relationship between auditory hallucinations and spontaneous fluctuations of skin conductance in schizophrenia. Brit J Psychiatr 142:47–52, 1983

Domino EF, Ruffing MD: Evidence for opioids as partial antagonists for indole hallucinogens. Psychopharm Bull, 18:175–179, 1982

Feder R: Auditory hallucinations treated by radio headphones. Am J Psychiatry 139:1188–1190, 1982

Fischer R: Prediction and measurement of perceptual–behavioral change in drug-induced hallucinations, in Origin and Mechanisms of Hallucinations. Edited by Keup W. New York, Plenum, 1970, 303–332

Fischman LG: Dreams, hallucinogenic drug states and schizophrenia: a psychological and biological comparison. Schizophr Bull 9:73–94, 1983

Freedman DX: Effects of LSD-25 on brain serotonin. J Pharmacol Exp Ther 134:160–166, 1961

Garralda ME: Hallucinations in children with conduct and emotional disorders: I. the clinical phenomena. Psychol Med 14:589–596, 1984a

Garralda ME: Hallucinations in children with conduct and emotional disorders: II. the follow-up study. Psychol Med 14:597–604, 1984b

Garralda ME: Psychotic children with hallucinations. Br J Psychiatry 145:74–77, 1984c

Heilbrun AB, Blum N: Cognitive vulnerability to auditory hallucination: impaired perception of meaning. Br J Psychiatry 144:508–512, 1984

Heilbrun AB, Blum N, Haas M: Cognitive vulnerability to auditory hallucination: preferred imagery mode and spatial localization of sounds. Br J Psychiatry 143:294–299, 1983

Heym J, Rasmussen K, Jacobs B: Some behavioral effects of hallucinogens are mediated by a postsynaptic serotonergic action: evidence from single unit studies in freely moving cats. Eur J Pharmacol 101:57–68, 1984

Hofman A: How LSD originated. Journal of Psychedelic Drugs 11:53–60, 1979

Hollister LE: Drug-induced psychoses and schizophrenic reactions, a critical comparison. Ann NY Acad Sci 96:80–88, 1962

Hollister LE: Chemical psychoses. Springfield, Illinois, Charles C Thomas, 1968

Horowitz MJ: Image formation and cognition. New York, Appleton-Century-Crofts, 1970

Horowitz MJ: A cognitive model of hallucinations. Am J Psychiatry 132:789–795, 1975

Jacobs BL, Trulson ME: Dreams, hallucinations and psychosis—the serotonin connection. Trends in Neuroscience 2: 276–280, 1979

Johnson MK, Raye CL: Reality monitoring. Psychol Rev 88:67–85, 1981

Kluver H: Mescal: The Divine Plant and Its Psychological Effects. London, K Paul, Trench, Tribner, 1928

Knauer A, Maloney WJM: A preliminary note on psychic action of mescaline with special reference to the mechanism of visual hallucinations. J Nerv Ment Dis 40:425–436, 1913

Launay G, Slade PD: The measurement of hallucinatory predisposition in male and female prisoners. Personality and Individual Differences 2:221–234

Margo A, Hemsly DR, Slade PD: The effects of varying auditory input on schizophrenic hallucinations. Br J Psychiatry 139:122–127, 1981

McCall RB, Aghajanian GK: Hallucinogens sensitize serotonin and norepinephrine receptors in the facial motor nucleus. Life Sci 26:1149–1156, 1980

Meltzer HY, Arora RC, Jackman H, et al: Platelet monoamine oxidase and plasma amino oxidase in psychiatric patients. Schizophr Bull 6:213–219, 1980

Mintz S, Alpert M: Imagery vividness, reality testing and schizophrenic hallucinations. J Abnorm Psychol 79:310–316, 1972

Nelson D: Central serotonergic receptors: evidence for heterogeneity and characterization by ligand-binding. Neurosci Biobehav Rev 6:499–502, 1982

Posey TB, Losch ME: Auditory hallucinations of hearing voices in 375 normal subjects. Imagination, Cognition and Personality 3:99–113, 1983

Rothlin E: Pharmacology of lysergic acid diethylamide and some of its related compounds. J Pharm Pharmacol 9:569–587, 1957

Slade PD: An investigation of psychological factors involved in the predisposition to auditory hallucinations. Psychol Med 6:123–132, 1976a

Slade PD: Towards a theory of auditory hallucinations: outline of an hypothetical four-factor model. British Journal of Social and Clinical Psychology 15:415–423, 1976b

Spanos NP, Stam HJ: The elicitation of visual hallucinations via brief instructions in a normal sample. J Nerv Ment Dis 167:488–494, 1979

Trulson ME, Jacobs BL: LSD acts synergistically with serotonin depletion: evidence from behavioral studies in cats. Pharmacol Biochem Behav 4:231–234, 1976

Trulson ME, Jacobs BL: Effects of 5-methoxy-N, N-dimethyltryptamine on behavior and raphe unit activity in freely-moving cats. Eur J Pharmacol 54:43–50, 1979a

Trulson ME, Jacobs BL: Long-term amphetamine treatment decreases brain serotonin metabolism: implications for theories of schizophrenia. Science 205:1295–1297, 1979b

Trulson ME, Heym J, Jacobs BL: Dissociations between the effects of hallucinogenic drugs on behavior and raphe unit activity in freely-moving cats. Brain Res 215:275–293, 1981

West LJ: A general theory of hallucinations and dreams, in Hallucinations. Edited by West LJ. New York, Grune & Stratton, 1962, 275–291

Young BG: A phenomenological comparison of LSD and schizophrenic states. Br J Psychiatry 124:64–73, 1974

Young JG: Methylphenidate-induced hallucinosis: case histories and possible mechanisms of action. Dev Behav Ped 2:35–37, 1981

Zigler E: Hallucinations vs. delusions: a developmental approach. J Nerv Ment Dis 171:141–146, 1983

Hallucinations in Children: A Psychoanalytic Perspective

Daniel Pilowsky, M.D.

5

Hallucinations in Children: A Psychoanalytic Perspective

Numerous authors have discussed the psychodynamic functions served by hallucinations (Eisenberg 1962; Simonds 1975; Weiner 1961; Wilking 1966), and a recent review (Rothstein 1981) summarizes the different viewpoints. Psychodynamically oriented researchers have devised numerous classifications. Each classification emphasizes a different aspect. Some authors emphasize form and content (Lukianowicz 1969; Simonds 1975); psychological structure, that is, id functions, ego functions, and superego functions (Modell 1958); primary versus secondary hallucinations (Weiner 1961); aims, degree of insight, and age at the onset of the hallucinations (Lukianowicz 1969); type, that is, auditory, visual, and tactile; affective tone (for example, "reassuring voices"); and desirability of hallucinations (Simonds 1975).

It is possible only to review the most frequently used classifications here. Weiner's primary hallucinations occur in the absence of a specifically diagnosable disease. His secondary hallucinations occur in the course of obvious organic and functional syndromes such as organic brain disease, epilepsy, and schizophrenia. Lukianowicz coined the term *aims of hallucinations*. He refers to aims such as escape mechanism, wish-fulfilling mechanism, neurotic reliving of a traumatic event, and so forth.

It is clear that these numerous classifications consist of largely overlapping categories. It is also relevant to mention that the various categories are poorly defined. Therefore, their usefulness is limited. It is suggested here that these classifications can be profitably integrated by considering two vantage points: that of the structural theory and that of the object relations and interpersonal points of view. These two vantage points lead to two classification schemes, which will be reviewed after a brief discussion of the role of a few general factors that may predispose a child toward hallucinating.

Among the general factors that may predispose a child, deprivation and various ego failures appear to be prominent. The role of deprivation is probably the most emphasized predisposing factor in the literature on hallucinations in children (Bender 1954; Bender and Lipkowitz 1940; Sachs 1962; Wilking 1966).

Wilking (1966, p 432) suggested that "deprivation seems to serve as an essential background for the failures in ego and superego development characteristic of many children in this group." She studied a group of deprived children in Harlem, New York City, and found a high incidence of hallucinatory experiences. Dr. Wilking suggests that these deprived children present failures of development in many areas; that is, there is little neutralization of aggression, there is an unresolved ambivalence in their object relations, impulse control is often poor, and the internalization of the superego is incomplete. Even though the concept of deprivation is widely used in our literature, its meaning often remains unclear. The term *deprivation* is used to refer to economic deprivation, emotional deprivation, and verbal deprivation. It is often unclear to which type of deprivation the different authors are referring. There is also confusion about the following issues in relation to deprivation: First, what minimal experiences during childhood are sufficient and necessary for normal psychological development? Second, are there critical periods in development during which insufficient exposures to certain experiences may have lasting consequences? Third, what minimal compensatory experiences may alleviate the psychological damage resulting from early deprivation? These issues were recently reviewed by Skuse (1984a, 1984b).

Given the numerous problems and ambiguities intrinsic to the concept of deprivation, it is difficult at this point to critically assess its role in the genesis of hallucinations in children. Furthermore, most of the published studies of hallucinations in children were done in hospitals that care primarily for deprived children in poor urban areas. The number of studies of children of higher socioeconomic status is small.

In addition to deprivation, several other general predisposing factors have been proposed: lower intelligence; hypercathexis of a particular mode of perception (visual, auditory, and tactile) because of individual life experiences; stress in the child's life; acceptance in the family of various religious and quasi-mystical experiences (Aug and Ables 1971; Bender 1954; Bender and Lipkowitz 1940; Eisenberg 1962; Wilking 1966); and poor body boundary demarcation (Fisher 1962).

STUDY OF HALLUCINATIONS FROM A STRUCTURAL PERSPECTIVE

Several authors (for example, Rothstein 1981; Wilking 1966) have proposed that hallucinations be classified in terms of the three psychic structures.

Hallucinations as an Expression of Superego Function

These usually are auditory hallucinations. The voices, which are often described as an externalized conscience, threaten to punish the child, warn him or her not to be bad, or belittle the child for some type of impulsive or destructive behavior. This type of hallucination is very common in clinical practice, often reflecting the presence of a punitive, rigid, and primitive superego. It has been suggested that in some cases, particularly when the parents are abusive or very critical, the occurrence or the content of the hallucinations may reflect the internalization of a punitive parental object.

Modell (1958), in a frequently quoted article, discussed in some detail the relationship between hallucinatory phenomena in schizophrenics and the supergego. The subjects he studied were hospitalized adult chronic schizophrenics. He pointed out that Freud (1914/1948) did not consider the hallucinated voices to represent the superego itself. Freud, instead, according to Modell, suggested that the appearance of voices reflects the regressive undoing of the superego. Modell quotes one of Freud's statements regarding hallucinations in support of his contention: "The voices as well as the indefinite number of speakers are brought into the foreground again by the disease, and so the evolution of conscience is regressively reproduced" (Freud, 1914/1948, p 30).

Before the formation of the superego, the child's prohibitions are external, that is, parental. The prohibitions later become internalized. With the emergence of the accusatory voices, the internalized prohibitions are now again perceived as arising from external sources. Therefore, Modell suggests, the voices reflect a stage in the prehistory of the superego but are not the superego itself. The superego of the early latency child contains prohibitions that have only recently, and sometimes only partially, been internalized. Therefore, the kind of regressive transformation of the superego described by Modell is to be frequently expected in this age group. The literature contains numerous examples of the phenomenon in latency-age children (see Bender 1954; Wilking 1966). The following description of one of Bender's examples illustrates the regressive transformation of the superego in a latency-age child.

Case Study 1

V. was an eight-year-old boy whose father was in jail. The father was a criminal, an alcoholic, and a drug addict. V. remembered the brutal beatings the father gave the mother before he was jailed. V.'s mother worked and he was cared for by his grandmother. He was also very close to an aunt who died of tuberculosis. After the aunt's death, V. started hearing her voice telling him to be good and to obey his mother's instructions and orders. The voice also told him that he wanted to lie, steal, and curse, and do other bad things that showed he was like his father. This boy was hospitalized, and the voices disappeared in the hospital environment.

This example shows how this boy, overwhelmed by his impulses, experienced a regression of the superego while living in a depriving environment. He was able to give up the hallucinations once he was placed in a more supportive environment that helped him control his impulses. The presence of an internalized punitive parental object is also demonstrated here.

Hallucinations as an Expression of Ego Function

Modell suggests that hallucinations in adult schizophrenic patients are often an expression of integrative ego functions: "The voices reviving as they do the wished-for parental relationships assume certain functions which at one time may have been assumed by the parents, functions which later became incorporated into the sphere of the ego's activity" (Modell 1958, pp 452–453). Modell gives examples of patients whose hallucinated voices were the source of such advice. The voices told one of Modell's patients how to cook and sew and gave the patient shopping advice. The same patient heard prohibitions and advice from two different voices or from one voice. In such cases the difficulty in differentiating the ego from the superego processes is evident.

Others (Bender and Lipkowitz 1940; Esman 1962) have described hallucinations that reflect attempts at mastery or gaining satisfaction in adaptive or partially adaptive ways as an expression of ego functions. At times hallucinations are described as an attempt at restitution. For example, the projection of a destructive parental introject, which is then perceived as a hallucination, may serve such a function. Esman describes two cases, one of which is presented below, where children projected their destructive parental introjects as an attempt at restitution.

Case Study 2

D., a six-year-old black boy, was admitted to the hospital following an acute hallucinatory episode involving the perception of a butterfly. This visual hallucination occurred after his mother had slapped him in the face with a wet washcloth because he failed to tie his shoes. He saw a shadow that later became a butterfly. He was extremely anxious. He feared that the butterfly was going to take his clothes off. In his play he often displayed anxiety while removing parts from toys and dolls.

D. was born out of wedlock to his 33-year-old mother. His mother's initial reaction to him was negative. He was hyperactive from infancy. When D. was 12 months old, his mother was hospitalized for the removal of a fibroid tumor. D. was boarded out from 12 to 16 months of age, and after his return home he had numerous nightmares, which increased in frequency at age 4 years following the birth of a younger brother. D.'s mother reported that she was sure he did not masturbate because "he knows I wouldn't let him get away with it."

D.'s hallucinations disappeared after a few days in the hospital, and he was discharged to his mother's care with outpatient follow-up.

The acute onset of his symptoms can be traced back to an emergence of rage directed at the mother. Had the child become conscious of his enormous rage, overwhelming anxiety and guilt would have arisen. Instead he defensively projected his rage in the form of a symbolic representation—a butterfly—of the introjected parental image, that is, his aggressive, castrating mother. Thus D. responded to the anxiety-laden situation with an acute regressive reaction, which constitutes an attempt at restitution involving the projection of a destructive parental object.

Hallucinations as an Expression of Id Function

Some authors refer to this group of hallucinations as an expression of libidinal and aggressive drives. The content of these hallucinations may refer to libidinal impulses, or aggressive impulses, or fear when the aggression is turned against the self. Typically they involve the projection of unacceptable sexual and aggressive impulses. They often consist of voices, such as the voice of the devil commanding the child to act out the unacceptable impulses. For example, a child may say that the voice of the devil told him to kill or hurt his or her mother. Such a child may verbalize or act out the aggressive intentions while disowning or disclaiming them.

Several authors have described cases of hallucinations that are seen as a libidinal discharge process (Katan 1950, 1952), or as the combinations of libidinal wishes and fears of the fulfillment of these wishes (Brenner 1951). Katan studied Schreber's hallucinations and suggested that Schreber's hallucinations represent a discharge of homosexual libido. Brenner studied the case of a three-and-a-half-year-old girl who presented terrifying visual hallucinations. Brenner suggested that the hallucinations of his patient represented a wish for, and a fear of, phallic penetration by the father.

There are also numerous examples in the literature of children and adolescents whose hallucinations represent a discharge of aggressive impulses. The following case was seen by the present author.

Case Study 3

A., a 14-year-old black female, was admitted to the hospital shortly after she attempted to poison her mother. A. put boric acid in her mother's tea after her mother had slapped her in the face. The mother had become enraged after she found out that A. had been truant from school for several days. A.'s mother, Mrs. C., was an angry, paranoid young woman who felt constantly persecuted by the powers that be. I interviewed A. following her admission to an inpatient unit in a city hospital. A. reported that she heard the voice of an "imaginary friend," who told her to poison her mother. After a brief discussion it became clear that A. believed in the actual existence of the imaginary friend. However, she referred to the friend as imaginary because she did not want to be labeled as "crazy." I pointed out to A. that she heard the voice telling her to kill her mother after the mother had slapped her in the face and suggested that she probably was furious at her mother at the time. A. refused to acknowledge the connection and kept repeating that she did what the voice told her to do. She proceeded to tell me that the voice had issued a new command: to break her mother's arm. A. spoke with a flat affect about poisoning her mother. I was unable to perceive any change in her voice or her face while she described her matricidal impulses.

This case illustrates how this adolescent discharged her aggressive impulses toward a parental object in response to a command hallucination. A. attempted to kill her mother while disclaiming her homicidal impulses through the use of a defensive projection.

It is suggested here that this projection includes previous introjects
of punitive parental objects.

STUDY OF HALLUCINATIONS FROM THE OBJECT-RELATIONS AND INTERPERSONAL VIEWPOINTS

From the object-relations viewpoint, the hallucinatory experiences
may be seen as an expression of internalized objects. There is some
overlap between the object-relations and structural viewpoints. For
example, the hallucinations described in Case Study 3 may be
described as id hallucinations, insofar as aggressive impulses are
reflected. They can also be seen, from an object-relations vantage
point, as the reflection of a "bad object," that is, a punitive parental
object. The object-relations viewpoint, I suggest, enriches the interpretation of the clinical data. Modell (1962) studied hallucinatory
phenomena from both the structural and the object-relations
points of view and published an intensive study of a small number
of hallucinating adult schizophrenics. He suggested that his patient's hallucinations were an expression of internalized parental
representations distorted by instinctual wishes. My own clinical
experience has led me to believe that in many cases hallucinations
of a sadistic and punitive character may be observed in children
whose parents are or had been actually abusive or extremely
punitive. In such cases the internalized parental representations
may constitute relatively undistorted reflections of the abusive or
punitive parents. A case reported by Aug and Ables (1971) illustrates this point: A 13-year-old girl became pregnant as a result of
an incestuous relationship with her father. When the pregnancy
was discovered, the father was sent to jail. He then threatened that
he would soon get out of jail and kill the child and her mother.
Shortly after the father was placed in jail, the child began to have
visual hallucinations. She saw the father appearing at the foot of
her bed, glowering at her in a very threatening way. These hallucinations are a reflection of a largely undistorted parental representation of a father who had acted out his sexual and aggressive
impulses toward his daughter. The patients described by Modell
are adult schizophrenic patients. Aug and Ables's patient, on the

other hand, was a nonpsychotic child who presented with hallucinations. The possibility that nonpsychotic children may express through their hallucinations relatively undistorted parental representations, and that schizophrenic patients' hallucinations may reflect more distorted parental representations, is a hypothesis worth studying.

Will (1962) studied the hallucinations of adult schizophrenics within the context of interpersonal psychoanalysis. He suggested that the "content of the hallucinations is composed of symbolic representations of previous interpersonal experience" (p 180). Applying this perspective to the hallucinations of nonpsychotic children, such hallucinations may be seen as representations of past or current interpersonal experiences that, in contrast to what happens in schizophrenic patients, have not been symbolized.

Will (1962, p 1745) suggested that when a person is hallucinating he or she "becomes cognizant of ideas which previously have not been clearly in his awareness, and may be thought of as having been dissociated." He goes on to suggest that the dissociated ideas are symbols of past interpersonal events that threatened the status of the organism through the arousal of anxiety. The individual is thus protected insofar as some feeling of security can be so maintained. Of course this feeling of security is maintained at the expense of distorting reality. This formulation follows Sullivan's (1953) view of psychopathology.

Will describes three types of experiences that may lead a child to dissociate. In the first of these experiences the child is exposed to conflicting messages by his or her caretakers. There is one message at the verbal level and an opposite message at a nonverbal level. For example, the child's mother says "I love you," but she says it with a tone of voice that indicates disgust. Second, "if a significant interpersonal experience (as with a parent) is attended by marked anxiety to which the child can not respond by avoidance or defensive maneuver, threatening aspects of the relationship may be dissociated" (Will 1962, p 176). Third, Will also claimed that olfactory, gustatory, and tactile experiences are often dissociated because they are considered, in certain cultures, as unsuitable to the adult way of life.

Will's formulation is particularly attractive because he attempts to explain why a child may need to hallucinate; that is, he mentions explicitly what kind of experience might lead to dissociations that later may be manifested as hallucinations. Of course, the type of experiences that he describes are found also in children who do not hallucinate and cannot always be demonstrated in children who hallucinate.

It is worth mentioning that the same type of hallucinations that may be seen as a reflection of parental introjects may also be seen, from a structural viewpoint, as a reflection of id, ego, or superego structures. A typical case is that of a father who is aggressive and sexually abusive yet can also be nurturing and give advice. The resulting parental introject may be seen as: a) a source of hallucinations of an aggressive and/or libidinal content; b) a source of hallucinations of parental prohibitions, that is, superego hallucinations; and c) a source of hallucinations that combine parental prohibitions and parental advice, that is, ego and superego hallucinations. This description is, of course, oversimplified because the term *internal objects*, as used in object-relations theory, does not refer to mirror images of the parental objects but to a variety of distorted and compensatory internal images. Therefore, several other possibilities, in addition to the three mentioned above, may be suggested, such as hallucinations that reflect the wished-for father or reflect any number of compensatory, distorted, or idealized parental images.

Finally, it is worth mentioning that Brenner (1951) cautions us against postulating that all hallucinations in children result from "bad" parental introjects or from an inadequate or depriving environment. He describes a case where the hallucinations' origins are in the child's own libidinal wishes and fears. In Brenner's case, both the parents and the environment are described as adequate.

As an example of a special case of internalized objects in children, Furer (1957) described a group of children who located the source of the hallucinations within their own body. These children often stated that they had the devil and an angel or god within themselves, within the abdomen or the chest or the head. Furer referred to these phenomena as "internalized hallucinations," and suggested that the voices correspond to introjected parental objects. Furer pointed out two intriguing findings: a) all the cases that demonstrated these internalized hallucinations were cases of schizophrenic children, and b) this type of hallucination was found to be more frequent among young schizophrenic children than among schizophrenic adolescents. He suggested that as these children mature, they project these hallucinations away from their own body and into the environment.

SUMMARY

Hallucinations have been classified from numerous theoretical perspectives. It is suggested that two of these views may be used to integrate the classifications: a) the structural and b) the object-relations and interpersonal. The object-relations and the interpersonal vantage points have been considered jointly here because there is a great deal of overlap insofar as childhood hallucinations are concerned. It is not implied, though, that object-relations theory and interpersonal theory are equivalent, or even that they can be integrated. That controversy is beyond the scope of this chapter.

References

Aug R, Ables B: Hallucinations in nonpsychotic children. Child Psychiatry Hum Dev 1:153–167, 1971

Bender L: Hallucinations in children, in A Dynamic Psychopathology of Childhood. Edited by Bender L. Springfield, Illinois, Charles C Thomas, 1954, 16–50

Bender L, Lipkowitz H: Hallucinations in children. Am J Orthopsychiatry 10:471–490, 1940

Brenner C: A case of childhood hallucinosis. Psychoanal Study Child 6:235–243, 1951

Eisenberg L: Hallucinations in children, in Hallucinations. Edited by West LJ. New York, Grune & Stratton, 1962

Esman A: Visual hallucinosis in young children. Psychoanal Study Child 17:334–343, 1962

Fisher S: Body image boundaries and hallucinations, in Hallucinations. Edited by West LJ. New York, Grune & Stratton, 1962

Freud S: On narcissism: an introduction in Collected Papers, vol 4. London, Hogarth Press, 1948, 30

Furer M: Internalized objects in children. Am J Orthopsychiatry 27:88–95, 1957

Katan M: Schreber's hallucinations: the little men. Int J Psychoanal 31:32–35, 1950

Katan M: Further remarks about Schreber's hallucinations. Int J Psychoanal 33:119–128, 1952

Lukianowicz N: Hallucinations in nonpsychotic children. Psychiatr Clin (Basel) 2:321–337, 1969

Modell A: The theoretical implications of hallucinatory experiences in schizophrenia. J Am Psychoanal Assoc 6:442–440, 1958

Modell A: Hallucinations in schizophrenic patients and their relation to psychic structure, in Hallucinations. Edited by West LJ. New York, Grune & Stratton, 1962

Rothstein A: Hallucinatory phenomena in childhood, a review of the literature. J Am Acad Child Psychiatry 20:623–635, 1981

Sachs L: Emotional acrescentism. J Am Acad Child Psychiatry 1:632, 1962

Simonds J: Hallucinations in nonpsychotic children and adolescents. Journal of Youth and Adolescence 4:171–182, 1975

Skuse D: Extreme deprivation in early childhood. I. diverse outcomes for three siblings from an extraordinary family. J Child Psychol Psychiatry 25:523–541, 1984a

Skuse D: Extreme deprivation in early childhood. II. theoretical issues
and a comparative review. J Child Psychol Psychiatry 25:543–572,
1984b

Sullivan HS: Conceptions of Modern Psychiatry. New York, WW Norton & Co, 1953

Weiner M: Hallucinations in children. Arch Gen Psychiatry 5:544–553,
1961

Wilking V: The hallucinatory experience: an attempt at a psychodynamic classification and reconsideration of its diagnostic significance. J
Am Acad Child Psychiatry 5:431–440, 1966

Will O: Hallucinations: comments reflecting clinical observations of the
schizophrenic reaction, in Hallucinations. Edited by West LJ. New
York, Grune & Stratton, 1962